RETHINK THE INTERNET

HOW TO MAKE THE DIGITAL WORLD A LOT LESS SUCKY

TRISHA PRABHU

PHILOMEL BOOKS

PHILOMEL BOOKS

An imprint of Penguin Random House LLC, New York

First published in the United States of America by Philomel Books,
an imprint of Penguin Random House LLC, 2022

Text copyright © 2022 by Trisha Prabhu

All photos courtesy of Trisha Prabhu.

Philomel Books is a registered trademark of Penguin Random House LLC.

Visit us online at penguinrandomhouse.com.

Library of Congress Cataloging-in-Publication Data is available.

Manufactured in Canada

ISBN 9780593352823

1 3 5 7 9 10 8 6 4 2

FRI

Edited by Jill Santopolo
Design by Monique Sterling
Text set in Freight Text Pro

To my parents, Bhanu and Neel Prabhu, who instilled in me the courage to dream of a better internet

And to my late grandmother, Shanta Sundari, my greatest inspiration

WELCOME TO THIS BOOK:

MEET ME, TRISHA PRABHU

Hey, there! What's up? Welcome to this book! You might be here for many reasons: (1) you think the internet is kinda sucky (I couldn't agree more) and you want to change it, (2) you want to learn more about the internet and technology (which, even though it's everywhere, is still kinda complicated . . .), or (3) . . . let's be real: some adult you know bought this book for you. Whichever of the three it is (and maybe it's more than one), I'm so excited you're here! Here's what that adult didn't know when they bought this book: I'm a young person, too, so I hate the lecturing, cringey, sappy "life lessons" just as much as you do. Let me start, then, by being clear: that's not what this book is about. It's also not here to make you use your phone a certain way, or to claim that technology is "bad." (Straight up, the only folks who think that are . . . well, old people.)

With all of that said, what *is* this book about? And why should you read it? Simply put, this book is designed to be an internet "survival guide." In this book, you'll find everything you need to know to be a successful digital citizen (and if you're wondering what that is, take a peek at chapter 1). Today's internet might seem pretty simple: hop online, chat with friends, watch videos, do your homework . . . but the internet—and technology more broadly—is much messier than you might realize. This book is meant to teach you seven main skills, which, if you master them, will ensure that the internet *never* gets the better of you. In other words, you can use tech to be awesome, instead of running into trouble you later regret.

Okay, maybe I have your attention. But if I were you, I'd still be kinda skeptical: *Who is this girl? And why does she get to teach me how to use the internet?* Good questions. That's what this part of the book is for. To get to know me, your internet instructor: the one, the only, the myth, the legend . . . Okay, I'm not *that* cool, so I'll skip the dramatic intro—my name is Trisha Prabhu, and I'm here to teach you how to do the internet right.

I'm originally from Illinois. I was born in Arlington Heights, which is a city in the suburbs of Chicago. My parents, Neel and Bhanu Prabhu, immigrated to the United States from India in the 1990s. A few years after they met, they got married, and in May 2000, the world was forever changed: *dramatic pause* I was born. A couple years later, we moved to the city I now call my hometown: beautiful Naperville, Illinois, another suburb of Chicago.

It was in Naperville that I first started to make friends, find interests, and, well, become who I am! Of course, my interests changed just as quickly as I did. At six, I wanted to be a queen—and command folks to make my favorite foods all day long (I can't lie, that's still what I want to be . . . but I know it's not going to happen. *Sigh*). At seven, I wanted to be an author (and will you look that—dreams do come true!). At eight, I wanted to be a basketball player, a sport I then played competitively. I dreamed of joining the WNBA, where I hoped to play as a power forward! And at nine, I wanted to be the president of the United States. It was around that age that I started to think more critically about the world's issues: global warming, gender equality, promoting kindness and respect. And it was then that I realized: When adults asked me what I wanted to be when I grew up, I didn't *really* know, but I did know that whatever I did, I wanted to solve important problems. I wanted to make change. I wanted to make an impact.

And then, at ten, perhaps the most important thing to ever happen to me happened: I was introduced to the incredible world of computers and coding! For those of you who don't know, computer programming, or "coding" as it's more informally called, is basically the act of talking to a computer. You can almost think of it as speaking in a foreign language—the language of computers! Whether you want to build a website

3

dedicated to cat memes or a social media app for Michael Jordan fans, you need to be able to tell your computer what it should create—but unfortunately, it doesn't know any human languages. Coding is what helps bridge the gap.

Rather quickly, I fell in love with coding. Why? Well, for one, as a kid I'd always hated math (argh), and coding was the first logical, quantitative thing I really enjoyed. For another, it was so awesome to actually be able to build a piece of technology, technology that people around the world could see and use. It truly was the best feeling: I'd always end a coding session feeling powerful and engaged. In any case, it was soon pretty clear: this wasn't going to be a hobby or a phase; it was going to be something I did for the rest of my life.

When I turned eleven, other things in my life started to change—and unfortunately, not for the better. I found myself embroiled in "girl drama" at school—something, I imagine, many of you might be familiar with (take it from me: it gets better). Apparently, my friends didn't think I was "cool enough" anymore. Without warning, I found myself without real friends, support, or anyone who truly liked me for me. I'd often eat lunch with my teachers, which, apart from being super embarrassing, actually ended up being a blessing: with them, I found a lot of solace.

Unfortunately, things only got bumpier from there: My former friends started to tease and harass me—excluding me, talking about me behind my back, and even playing tricks on me. My phone, which I'd gotten just a little while before, ended up being a big part of it: I'll never forget the day I got a text from someone I *thought* was my crush. Eagerly, I responded, thrilled that they'd gotten my number—and were texting me! I was on cloud nine . . . but I wasn't there for long. Later that day, I learned that those texts were never actually from my crush; in fact, it'd been three girls from my school, including two of my former friends, pranking me. They seemed to think it was hilarious, but I was crushed—and felt like an idiot. I didn't think it could get worse, until the next day, when I arrived at school and found them showing my classmates screenshots of our texts. "She's so lame," I heard one girl say. "Yeah," the girl next to her agreed. "This is literally pathetic. Did she really think he would be interested?" They all laughed. Funnily enough, when they realized I was standing there, they hastily stuffed their phones away and fell silent, masking their smiles. One even complimented me. "Wow, Trisha! I love that skirt." The others nodded. I remember realizing: *it's not that they don't know that what they're doing is wrong . . . just that somehow, on a phone, it's easier for them to be cruel, unkind, and mean.*

It was a tough period for me. I don't know if you've ever felt this way, but back then, I often felt like the world was my mirror: things people said about me stuck with me and would influence how I saw myself. I started to believe those girls—maybe I was lame, pathetic, imperfect, and unwanted. I lost a lot of my confidence, my spirit, and the positivity that was once integral to my personality. And more than anything, I *hated* my phone: a constant reminder that I just wasn't good enough, whatever "good enough" was.

Maybe you've been through something similar to what I went through, or maybe you're lucky enough to have avoided some of the worst of middle school (once again, I swear: it gets better). In any case, you have to agree: middle school isn't the only problem here . . . As those girls demonstrate, a sucky internet is definitely part of it too.

At first, I didn't think about it that way. Thanks to that "mirror" effect, I thought there was something wrong with *me*, that I was the only one who'd ever been bullied or harassed like that. It was only a few years later, at thirteen, when I realized that that couldn't be further from the truth. One day after I came home from school, I was browsing the internet and stumbled upon a story about Rebecca Sedwick, a twelve-year-old girl from Florida. The article said she'd been cyberbullied for over a year and a half, after which she dropped out of school and suffered from serious mental health issues that caused her death by suicide. I was shocked; it seemed unreal to think that kids were being driven out of school and even killed because of what they'd been sent on social media! I immediately started to do more research—and that's when, for the first time, I learned about the scope of this issue: every day, millions of young people around the world receive mean or hurtful messages on the internet . . . partly because, well, it's just so easy to be mean online. Technology, it seemed, was enabling the spread of hate at pandemic proportions.

I was shocked—and fired up. You know that feeling when, well . . . you just *have* to do something about a problem? That's how I felt. I couldn't let this go; I refused to let a sucky internet reign even a minute longer! Somehow, someway, I pledged to myself, I was going to fix this thing. (Cue the heroic Disney music!)

That left me with just one important question to answer: How the heck was I actually going to do that? I was a teenager, with no resources, experience, background, or skills. *Except— Wait!* I quickly realized that that wasn't true: *I have the all-powerful skill of coding!* And so—contrary to most anti-hate work to date—I started to seriously think about how I could use technology to solve this issue, an issue that technology itself created.

After months of brainstorming, building, and experimentation, I had the answer, and my solution, which I named "ReThink," was born. The concept was simple: I knew that a lot of young people (myself included!) were prone to making rash, sometimes silly decisions—and it's not all our fault (at this age, our brains aren't actually designed to be super thoughtful). I hypothesized that that effect could've possibly translated to the internet: in other words, staring at a phone— rather than someone's face—made it even easier to let bad decision-making take over! What I wanted to create was a brake: something that would give a user a chance to pause, review, and rethink saying something mean, before the damage was done. I developed a vision: If someone tried to text me "I hate you!" their phone would receive an alert. HOLD UP! ARE YOU SURE YOU WANT TO SAY THAT? THAT'S NOT COOL. The technology could function as an app—an app that gave young people a chance to do the thing they already knew was right.

So that's exactly what I did: computer in hand, I got to work coding. I later found that the ReThink solution was extremely effective: almost everyone who received a chance to rethink a mean message changed their mind and decided not to say it! (Move over, Thomas Edison—there's a new inventor in the house.)

From there, my little idea ballooned into a global movement. A year later, I found myself running a company, giving talks about my work on stages around the world—from the White House to ABC's *Shark Tank*—and leading anti-hate awareness campaigns. Without meaning to, I'd stumbled upon a way to do what I'd always wanted to do—make an impact, especially on really important issues—and as a teenager, which was super awesome.

And that's how I find myself here, writing to all of you! In my many years of trying to fix this thing we call the internet, I've seen it all and learned a lot. And I want to share that knowledge—as well as my handy digital tricks and tips—with all of you.

Okay, Trisha, you might be thinking. *Seems like you know what you're talking about. But seriously, do I really need to read this book?*

The short answer? Yes. But I'm not sure that's satisfying, so here's the long answer: Our generation (sometimes referred to as "Gen Z") is the first to be born into a world of technology, but we won't be the last. Technology and the internet are here, and if you ask me, they're here to stay. And that's a good thing: For the most part, your phone, your computer, and the internet you access through those devices are great, right? You can learn about new topics, connect with friends, and even create some hilarious memes. But part of learning to live in a new society—in our case, a society that runs on technology—is ensuring that you're ready to be successful in that society. In the same way you go to school so that one day you can be successful in the "real world," you also need a digital education in order to be an "internet insider." Otherwise, the internet can—and most likely will—get the better of you, as it has so many people. And, well, that would be *really* sucky.

But don't worry, there's nothing to fear—Trisha is here! (Okay, that was kind of lame. But hey, it rhymed—give me some credit.) Jokes aside, I have your back. I'm here to teach you everything you need to know, in a format that's actually fun, interesting, and informative.

In the chapters that follow, you'll find seven stories that aim to teach you the seven skills you need to know to crush this thing we call our digital universe. Each story is paired with an Internet Challenge, so you can practice your new skills. Get ready to learn, laugh, and have a lot of fun!

I'll see you there—and I can't wait. Thanks again for joining me on this journey. Let's go!

Trisha Prabhu

CHAPTER 1
THE POST HEARD ROUND THE WORLD

When I got my first phone, I thought it was, well . . . just a phone! You probably do, too, but guess what? There's actually so much more to your phone than you might think. When you get your first phone, you don't just get a phone—you get a community. Who's in the group? Lots of other people from around the world, who also have phones (or computers, or tablets, or, potentially, a robot named Clyde)! It's simple: if you have a device, you're in the club. (If it helps, imagine that a superstrong force field binds all of you together!) Now that you're in, what are the rules? Well, being in this community is a pretty big responsibility: you have a duty to the other people in the group to be on your tiptop absolute best behavior. With so much power—every message you post can reach, impact, and influence all of those people—being a good digital citizen is one of the most important things you can do.

Melinda Skirt-Shirts's alarm rang. Most mornings, Melinda would groan, roll over, and pull the covers back up. But this morning, the day after Thanksgiving, Melinda jumped right out of bed. "Today's the day!" she said, humming to herself happily.

"Melinda!" she heard her mom call out from the kitchen. "We're leaving in fifteen minutes!"

"Okay, Mom!" Melinda called back. She quickly booted up her computer. A blinking icon—a pink purse—appeared: MELINDA'S LOOK OF THE DAY, it was labeled. She clicked on it.

Large block letters flashed on the computer screen. HELLO, MELINDA. GOOD MORNING, AND WELCOME TO YOUR LOOK. WHAT WOULD YOU LIKE TO TRY ON TODAY? The text disappeared, and a full-size image of Melinda appeared. "Yes!" Melinda said triumphantly. "It's working!" She'd been building this program for months, hoping it would be ready by today. Finally, her hard work had paid off!

At the top of her screen, a button appeared: TOPS. She clicked on it, and then on the red woolen sweater she'd been saving for a special occasion (RED WOOLEN SWEATER). She then clicked on BOTTOMS. Squinting, she scanned the options. *What would go well with this sweater?* And then it caught her eye: her lightly faded sky-blue jeans! She clicked on LHT BLUE FADE JEANS. The computer whirred. A few seconds later, a new image appeared: Melinda, with the outfit on. *It's perfect!* "Fashion mission accomplished!" Melinda said happily, dashing off to her closet.

When she had first run the "Look of the Day" idea by her two best friends, Priya Buttons and Mariana Cardigan, they did not get it. "Why do you actually need that?" Mariana had asked. *What they don't get,* Melinda thought now, *is just how long it takes to try on clothes—especially when you're a fashion queen!*

And that's exactly what Melinda was. For some kids, their passion was football; for other kids, it was music. For Melinda, it was fashion—and especially fashion design. Melinda didn't just buy clothes, she made her own. The red sweater was a Melinda Skirt-Shirts original™, the result of weeks of sketching, knitting, and last-minute alterations. One day, Melinda wanted to be a fashion designer in New York—or, as she put it on social media, a "#FashionBoss." She hoped to design everything from pants to bathing suits to shoes. Above all else, though, her dream project was a wedding dress. One day, she hoped, all of the wedding designs in her sketchbook—from the lace-covered dresses to the funky pink-and-white tie-dyed pantsuits—would be the hottest pieces out there.

To make that happen, though, Melinda needed to learn more, to see more, and to buy more. Which was why today was so special: It was Black Friday! The one day a year where everyone stopped, dropped, and shopped! With her mom as her personal consultant (and chauffeur), Melinda always visited all of the shops and boutiques in Fashiontowne. It was one of the few times she could (for the most part) afford everything on the shelves. From pants to shoes to jewelry, Melinda went bananas! She'd leave each store with bags full of items. This year, though, would be even better . . . because they were going to look for a wedding dress for her mom!

"Melinda!" her mom called again. "CutieShoes opens at seven. We're going to be late—let's go!"

"Coming!" Melinda called back. She grabbed her coat—a matching red, of course!—and phone. *Just one last thing to do!* It was time for her "Look of the Day" post. Angling her phone, she took a selfie just as the early morning light spilled into her bedroom. *Perfect.* She quickly posted it to her FashionGram (@Melinda Fashion Blog) with the caption: **Too cool 4 school on Black FriYAY! #BlackFridayLookOfTheDay #SoExcited**.

A few seconds later, her phone pinged. A new account, @Fashion4Fun, had followed her! A new comment on her selfie appeared: @Fashion4Fun: **Too cute!!! Omg I love!**

Melinda smiled. *The day is off to a great start!*

And it ended that way too—for Melinda, at least. Her shopping day was, by all accounts, a #HugeFashionSuccess. But her mother's was less so.

They'd gone to WeddingCarnival, DressGalore, and Dream-

Dress, but they couldn't find anything Melinda's mother liked. Melinda agreed—the dresses just weren't the right style. And her mom deserved the best!

"I was just thinking," her mom said as they packed Melinda's new clothes into the car. "What if—only if you want to—you designed and made my wedding dress? I'd pay you, of course, so it can be your first official sale. And there's nothing I'd rather wear more than a Melinda Skirt-Shirts original," she added, winking.

Melinda's heart leaped. *Oh. My. God! It's my dream, finally come to life!* Melinda immediately thought of her sketchbook, filled with her outlines of wedding dresses. *I can actually make one of those!* And this would be one of the most important wedding dresses of her lifetime—she'd be able to make something for her mom (and get paid)! *That means that you'll be an official designer, Melinda*, she thought. *I'm going to be an official designer!*

"So . . ." Melinda's mom glanced at her, smiling. "Is that a yes?"

Melinda squealed. "YES, yes, yes, yes! Thank you, thank you, thank you, Mom!" They both started to laugh.

On the rest of the way home, her mom continued to talk—about the wedding venue, the place cards, and the invitation list—but Melinda wasn't listening. There was only one thing on her mind: her mom's wedding dress.

Over the next week, Melinda obsessed over the dress. It was unlike any other piece she'd ever designed and made—*so it's going to be a ton of work.* To make matters worse, Melinda was, as they say, "#FashionBlocked." Inspiration refused to strike, and when an idea did come to her mind, it was never quite right. Day after day, she tried to finalize a design, but every time she thought she'd come to something, she was overcome with doubt. *It's too traditional. No, it's too outside the box. Is that lace cute, or is it old-fashioned? Will the material actually create those folds and creases? The dress will be worthless without them.* By the end of the week, she was completely panicked. If she didn't come to a design soon, she'd be late to buy the materials. And if she was late to buy the materials . . . her mom wouldn't have a dress on her wedding day!

Deep breaths, Melinda, she told herself. *You need to calm down.* To take her mind off the dress, she decided to join Mariana and Priya on a trip to the mall. There, inhaling the comforting smells of new clothes and perfumed stores, she shared her story of woe. "Y'all . . . what am I going to do?"

"To be honest, I can't believe you even agreed to do that," Mariana said, raising her eyebrows. "I could never. *Way* too much pressure."

"Mariana! Not helping," Priya said. "Don't worry, Mel." She linked her arm through Melinda's. "When you find the right design, you'll know. You just need a little . . . inspiration."

"Yeah, but how am I supposed to find some?" Melinda groaned. "I can't do this," she said dejectedly. "Maybe I should just give up."

"Hold on!" Mariana looked up. "You need inspiration, right?" Melinda nodded. "Uh—have you considered that we're literally swimming in it right now? Look around!" She gestured at the passersby in the mall. "There are a ton of looks here, and I'm sure you'll find ideas you can use for the dress. So take your cues from the good people of Fashiontowne!"

Priya cackled and shook her head. "Okay, serious ideas only, please. She's not going to get wedding-dress ideas from Mr. Tasteless," she said disdainfully. A few feet away, at the Fashiontowne Hot Dog Stand, Mr. Tasteless was grilling his famous hot dogs and burgers. His red sweater clashed horribly with his neon-yellow pants. *Argh.* "Speaking of which, I'm hungry!" Priya added.

"For the record, it *was* a serious idea! And you shouldn't be so dismissive; I'm pretty much a genius," Mariana declared.

Priya rolled her eyes.

"And oooh—I'm hungry too!" Mariana said. "I want a cheese dog. Melinda, are you coming?"

"I'm not hungry," Melinda said, waving her hands. "Go on."

"We'll be right back!" Priya said. She and Mariana dashed off.

Melinda sighed and glanced over at Mr. Tasteless. Eyeing his outfit, she did a double take. *Wait.* Upon second glance, Melinda realized she loved Mr. Tasteless's sweater, the knitted pattern in particular. *Sure, it looks pretty bad with the pants, but flying solo, and in an off-white color, it would*

be perfect for the skirt of the wedding dress, Melinda thought. Looking around, Melinda felt the realization dawning on her: *Mariana was right. There's inspiration everywhere!* Over at Candyland Candy Store, Mrs. O'Caramel donned a gorgeous white lace scarf. "That cut and color would look great on a veil," Melinda whispered. Instinctively, she grabbed her phone; zooming in on the scarf, she quickly snapped a picture.

Oh . . . argh! As she took the picture, Melinda realized she'd forgotten to post her "Look of the Day" on FashionGram! She'd been so preoccupied with the dress, it had completely slipped her mind. *I can't post a picture of myself now.* Her hair was a mess, and she still had chocolate on her mouth from the hot chocolate she'd bought a little while ago at CoffeeCafe. *What do I do?* Looking down at the photo of the scarf, Melinda suddenly had a great idea. *Bingo.* "Fashionbulb moment," she whispered.

She opened FashionGram and quickly typed out a caption. **Gorgeous white scarf @FashiontowneMall. 😜 Wish it was longer, though—and wrapped twice! #FashionLowdown #FashionReview**. She was about to post the picture of the scarf when she felt a pang of doubt. She'd never posted a picture of someone other than herself before. It felt a little . . . unsettling. She hesitated, and then, a few seconds later, finally hit POST.

Immediately, her phone began to buzz. The picture was blowing up; her followers loved the content. Her latest follower, @FASHION4FUN, commented, **I LOVE this take.** 💿😄

Keep the comments coming! Just a few minutes later, ten additional accounts had followed her.

Ideas for the wedding dress and more followers on FashionGram? I guess Mariana really is a genius, Melinda thought.

After Melinda got home, Mariana's idea was still on her mind . . . because everywhere she went, she saw ideas in people's outfits. At the grocery store, while her mom examined the farmstand veggies, Melinda was snapping pictures of Ms. Chococake, the head baker in the baked goods section, and her velvet skirt; at checkout, she took a shot of Adriana Popular's white halter top. *Ooh . . . what if the dress had a halter cut?* Every time she took a photo, she shared it on FashionGram, with a somewhat snarky caption. (**Spotted @ LocalGrocers. Velvet? Yikes. 😆 But the cut makes for an effortless look. Perfect for a wedding dress!**) *That's not so bad, right?* Each photo generated a ton of likes, comments, and followers—everyone absolutely loved this stuff! Melinda could see why; she had to admit to herself, compared to her "Look of the Day," this was *way* more fun. *And after all*, she thought, *the best fashion designers began as critics.* This was her fashion awakening!

The next day at school, when Melinda walked in, Priya and Mariana ran up to her. "Melinda! We saw the pictures. It's genius!" Mariana said triumphantly. "Or rather, as I said, I'm a genius!"

Priya's smile seemed forced, though, and she looked nervous. "What's wrong, Pri?" Melinda asked.

"Just be careful, Mel. I mean, some of the captions and comments are a little . . . I don't know." She hesitated. "Rude? I just don't want you to get in trouble." Internally, Melinda rolled her eyes. *Of course. Leave it to Miss Goody Two-Shoes Priya to ruin all the fun.*

"'Trouble'? You deserve an award." Mariana said, squeezing Melinda's hand. They both laughed.

Priya looked pained. "I have to go to first period," she said.

After she left, Mariana sighed and whispered to Melinda, "Ignore her, Mel."

Agreed, Melinda thought.

Throughout the day, Melinda took picture after picture of the students in her classes. Remy Dazzle's bedazzled belt was, as she said on FashionGram, a little #Extra, but it made Melinda think: *What if I cinched the wedding dress with a matching white belt?* In history class, Jack Fancy was in a suit for his book report presentation; as it turned out, he looked a lot like a younger version of Pat McTies, her future stepfather! *That's a great way to envision Pat's look at the wedding.* Every spare moment she got—whether at lunch or during free period—Melinda shared all of the shots on

FashionGram. Her account was ballooning; by the end of the day, she had five hundred new followers.

That evening, after she'd finished her homework, Melinda started working on a final sketch, sourcing colors, patterns, and design ideas from the pictures she'd taken. She felt herself buzz with creativity. *Finally*, she thought. *I found my groove.*

At that moment, her phone pinged. *Beep.* Melinda glanced at it but then shook her head. *Stay focused, Melinda. Stay in the zone.*

Beep.

Is that my phone again?! Melinda thought. *Ignore it, ignore it, ignore it.* But just as she'd refocused, her phone began to buzz wildly. *Beep. Beep. Beep. Beep.* "What's going on?" Melinda said out loud, confusedly grabbing her phone. *Ah.* It was FashionGram. "More followers?" Melinda whispered happily, opening the app.

After clicking on her profile, she gasped. *Oh my goodness . . . hold on. This can't be happening.* Her account was blowing up, and tons of people—including, she realized, a ton of folks from school, many of whom she didn't really know—were following her. She checked her follower status. *Three thousand new followers? No way.* That was when . . . *Beep.* @REMYDAZZZLE HAS FOLLOWED YOU! *Beep.* @FASHIONTOWNE-MALL HAS FOLLOWED YOU! *Beep.* @ADRIANAPOP HAS FOLLOWED YOU! Melinda felt her heart drop.

A few seconds later, a comment appeared. @REMYDAZZZLE: **@MelindaFashionBlog how dare you post this picture without asking me?! 😡 RUDE. I hope you get expelled!** Other followers liked the comment and added their own. (**Wait. You didn't ask before posting? 😲 Not cool. 🙄**)

An hour later, Melinda had dozens of angry messages from classmates, and even Ms. Chococake! "Dear Melinda," her message read. "It was incredibly inappropriate of you to take a picture of me without my permission and then share it on the internet with your critiques. I never asked for your comments."

Reading her note, Melinda felt herself shrink. *Priya was right*, Melinda realized. *I made a huge mistake. This is the worst fashion crisis ever.* Immediately, she deleted all of the pictures. *There. Problem solved . . . right?* For some reason, Melinda still couldn't shake feeling ashamed and regretful. What had she done?

As if on cue, the door hurled open. Startled, Melinda jumped and looked up from her phone. Standing in the doorway was her mom, glaring. *Uh-oh.* "I just got off a very interesting call with Principal Rule. Care to explain why there are pictures of *other people* on your FashionGram account, Melinda Leanne Skirt-Shirts?" she asked angrily, her voice rising.

"Mom, I can explain," Melinda said, her voice shaking. She took a deep breath. "I was just . . . I was struggling with the wedding dress. And I needed some ideas, so I took a few pictures. It wasn't that big of a deal! It's a . . . fashion-design thing." Her voice trailed off.

"Well, whatever *thing* it is, it's done now." Her mom's voice was frosty. "I appreciate the work you're putting into the dress, Melinda," she said, "but it's no excuse. If *this* is what it takes for you to make a wedding dress, then maybe you shouldn't be working on this project."

What?! Melinda thought. *No!* "It was just a few pictures!" she protested. "C'mon, Mom!"

"No, it wasn't, Melinda!" her mom replied. "Your phone isn't just about you."

Melinda paused, taking a second to think. *My mom is right,* she realized. *The things I said didn't just affect me, they affected other people too.* Deep down, she'd known that, but she'd ignored the truth . . . with #FashionDisaster consequences.

"I know you didn't mean to hurt anyone or violate their privacy, but intentions aside, that's what you did," her mom said.

Melinda looked away. "I should've asked first," she acknowledged.

Her mother nodded. "And if you're going to be a fashion critic, your followers, and the people you take pictures of, need to know that. Speaking of which, the best critics are not rude!"

Melinda sighed. "My followers loved it, though!" she said, thinking back to all of the likes and comments she'd received on FashionGram.

"It's not your followers you have to think about," her mom replied evenly. "Think about who you are, the person you want to be, and your responsibilities to your friends."

23

She shook her head. "I thought you were more mature than this. Clearly, I was wrong. I'm sorry . . . but I'm not sure you should work on the dress anymore, Melinda."

Not work on the dress? This can't be happening.

"Please, Mom!" Melinda was practically begging. "This dress . . . it means everything to me. And with everything changing . . . it's made me happy, you know? Please."

Her mom looked at her. Melinda could tell she was considering. "Fine. But on one condition."

"Anything!" Melinda said, relieved. "What is it?"

"That you make amends," her mom said firmly. Melinda nodded. *It's time to fix this.*

Over the next few days, Melinda got to work—not on the wedding dress, but on fixing the disaster she'd created. Within a few hours, she had an apology post up on Fashion-Gram. @MELINDAFASHIONBLOG: **To all of my followers and the FashionGram community, I'm so very sorry. In sharing the pictures I did, I violated the first rules of fashion creation: respect and positivity. As I've learned, those rules are doubly important in the fashion community.**

So right. Proud of you for recognizing this. ♥, @FASHION4FUN commented. Melinda also sent apology notes to each person she'd photographed. **It's ok and I appreciate this. Thks for the note!** Remy wrote back. **Thank you, Melinda**, Ms. Chococake replied. **I'm glad to see you've**

learned from this mistake. *That I have*, Melinda thought. *I'm never going to do this again.*

A few evenings later, apologies complete, Melinda opened up FashionGram. She felt much calmer scrolling through pictures now that her fashion debacle was finally over. *Until* . . . a picture she'd posted earlier that year caught Melinda's eye. It was one of her, Mariana, and Priya, from when they'd all dressed up as superheroes for Halloween; they were laughing so hard—about what, Melinda had forgotten. Suddenly, Melinda realized there was actually one last thing to do.

An hour later, she was outside Priya's door, a Fashiontowne hot dog in hand. Priya opened the door and squinted confusedly. "Melinda? What are you doing here?"

Melinda took a deep breath. "Pri, I'm really sorry about the pictures," she said. "You tried to warn me, and I should've listened to you. Instead, I was a terrible person. I was being a bad friend, and I feel horrible." She held up the hot dog. "Do you forgive me?" she asked nervously. *What if she says no?*

There was a short pause. Then Priya broke into a smile. "Of course, Mel. Best friends forever, right?" They hugged. Melinda felt herself sigh in relief. She could live without FashionGram, but she couldn't live without Mariana and Priya!

"And, for the record, you're not a terrible person," Priya said. "I gotta give Mariana credit—the idea wasn't all that bad, either. I think you just went about it in the wrong way," she said thoughtfully.

Wait, Melinda thought. "Fashionbulb moment," she whispered. "Pri?" she asked. "How would you like to be featured on my FashionGram? I want it to celebrate the looks and fashion I love, and your outfit looks incredible tonight." Priya brightened. "You can approve the picture and the caption, of course!"

"YES!" Priya squealed. "I want to be FashionGram famous!"

Melinda smiled. *Now that's a fashion mission accomplished!*

CHAPTER 1 INTERNET CHALLENGE

Congratulations on completing chapter 1! You've officially earned your "digital citizen" badge!

Melinda Skirt-Shirts is a very talented fashion designer, but, as we read, she definitely ran into some trouble on FashionGram! At the heart of her troubles was a lack of understanding around what makes a good digital citizen. As she—and hopefully you—learned, the internet isn't just about you: it's a community, and anything you say or do can reach a ton of people. Unfortunately, by sharing folks' pictures online without asking permission or thinking about how her comments could affect them, Melinda neglected her duty to her fellow digital citizens . . . without even trying! Ultimately, she avoided fashion crisis not by abandoning the idea completely—but by realizing that she needed to put respect and consideration for others at the center of her posts.

Now that you've read Melinda's story, it's time for you to take the reins as a budding digital citizen! As your first Internet Challenge, ask a friend's permission before you post a picture with them on a social media platform, and in the caption, explain why it's #AlwaysImportantToAsk. Tag five friends and ask them to do the same. See my selfie below for an example!

@TrishPrabhu: It was so great to hang out with my friend Nick today! 😄 As a part of an Internet Challenge, I made sure to ask before I posted . . . because it's #AlwaysImportantToAsk. What if he didn't like this filter?! Passing the challenge on to @Friend1, @Friend2, @Friend3, @Friend4, and @Friend5! Ask before you post—it's common courtesy, duh! 👋

CHAPTER 2
INTERNET PEOPLE ARE REAL PEOPLE TOO

H ave you ever said something you regretted? We've all had those moments—especially me! Maybe you're angry at your parents, frustrated that you didn't get a part in the school play, or tired after a long sports practice (or all three!), and suddenly, you say something terrible. It's usually not that creative, either, like "I hate you!" or "Go away, you moron!" (I'm guilty of having said both—and, at times, a lot worse.) Speaking personally, I always feel terrible after I say something like that. Unfortunately, from behind a phone screen, it's even easier to be your worst self, and your words can get away from you. When they do over and over again, it's called "cyberbullying." Cyberbullying is really sucky! Victims are hurt, and cyberbullies compromise on who they are and want to be—in other words, no one wins. Luckily, if you follow a simple mantra, you can keep yourself in check: **if you wouldn't say it to someone's face, don't say it online.** Internet people are real people too! When in doubt, choose kindness in everything you do.

Brody McNewKid looked out at what seemed like a sea of people. There were kids *everywhere*—jostling through the halls, opening lockers, running up to each other ("Oh my goodness—hi! How was your summer?"), and even throwing food at each other (yuck). *And they all seem to know each other*, Brody thought. *Great.* Earlier that year, when his dad had announced he'd received a big promotion and the family was moving to Washington, DC, Brody had prepared himself for (as his mom put it) "a whole new world." At that moment, though, looking out at the students at his new school— Newbie Middle School—he had never felt more homesick. *I wish I was back in Louisville.* There, the first day of school had always meant grits, gravy, and warm, buttery biscuits. Here, this morning his mom had tried to serve him some turkey bacon. "The neighbors recommended it!" his mom had said encouragingly. Now, thinking back on that first bite of turkey bacon, Brody shuddered. "Disgusting!" he muttered to himself, shaking his head.

"What was that, bud?" Brody's dad's voice interrupted his thoughts.

Brody looked up at his dad. "Nothing," he replied in monotone.

His dad put a hand on his shoulder and looked him square in the eyes. Brody knew what was coming: a classic "McNewKid moment," as his sister called it. "Hey—if you're nervous, it's okay. You know that, right?" Brody nodded. "Listen, I know it's going to be different," his dad said. "But it's also exciting! You'll get to meet new people and experience new things." Brody rolled his eyes. "Nuh-uh," his dad said, shaking his head. "I don't want to see any of that attitude." He grabbed Brody's hand. "Promise me you'll give it a chance."

Brody sighed. "Fine."

"Attaboy!" Brody's dad squeezed him as he pulled him in for a hug. "I'm proud of you, son." He looked down at his watch. "Crud. I gotta get going—I'll see you tonight; I can't wait to hear all about it!" A moment later, he was gone.

From behind him, Brody heard Principal Nosy ask gently, "Brody, are you ready to go to class?"

Brody nodded. "Yes, ma'am."

Principal Nosy smiled. "Wonderful. I see you have your schedule. It looks like you'll be starting in homeroom, and then off to first-period chemistry. And as I'm sure you can guess, from there just follow the list. And if you need help . . . well, my morning is relatively open, so I'm happy to walk you to class, help you get a lay of the land . . ." Behind her, Brody saw a few kids listening in at their lockers smirk.

"No!" Brody said quickly. "I mean, thank you so much,

Principal Nosy—I really appreciate that—but I'm sure I'll find my way." *I don't need the whole school thinking I'm a baby.*

Principal Nosy nodded. "All right, then, Brody. Have a great day." *We'll see about that*, Brody thought.

He looked out at the crowd of students again. *It's time for a new rodeo, McNewKid. Here we go.*

Unfortunately, the school building was much more confusing than Brody had anticipated. Nothing was in order! The *A* set of classrooms was followed by *G*, *D*, and *E*. "Who designed this building?" Brody said to himself angrily. By the time he finally made it to homeroom—after covertly consulting a teacher walking in the same direction—he was ten minutes late. He tried to explain to his homeroom teacher, Mr. Stricter, that it was all a mistake, but Mr. Stricter shook his head.

"We have a zero-tolerance tardy policy. You're tardy. Take a seat." He pointed to a desk at the front of the classroom.

Thanks for the warm welcome, Brody thought. When he took a seat, he heard a snicker. "Yo, McNewKid!" To his right, a big, burly boy stared at him, his face sneering. "That's your name, right?" Brody nodded. "Dude, *what's with the shoes*?" Next to him, three or four boys started to laugh. Brody stared down at his brown leather boots. *They were cool in Louisville.*

"Settle down over there," Mr. Stricter said absently, absorbed in the game he was playing on his phone.

As soon as the bell rang, Brody tore out of the classroom; he'd never wanted to leave a class more! As he walked to his next class, he felt his heart sinking. *This move was a terrible mistake*, he thought. *Why did Dad have to do this?* Looking down at his schedule, he grew more incensed. "I mean, what kind of school makes seventh graders take *chemistry*?" he said loudly. They only had one course—science—back in Louisville.

"I'm totally with you there, dude," a voice said. Brody jumped, startled. *What was that?*

"You okay?" The voice laughed. Brody turned. Standing next to him was a girl! Half of her hair was dyed purple, the other half green. Her T-shirt—which had the words BE DIF-FERENT written across it—was so long it reached her knees. And her eyes were a piercing black. *I've never seen anyone quite like this*, Brody thought apprehensively. With one hand on her hip, the girl looked him up and down, as if she were examining him. "I've never seen you around here. Who are you?"

"Hello there." Brody stuck out his hand. "My name is Brody McNewKid. And yeah—I'm new round here. My family just got up here from Louisville, Kentucky."

The girl laughed. "Whoa! Dude, your accent is serious." Brody looked down. *Great. Does everyone have to make fun of me?* The girl must've realized what he was thinking, because she smiled and said, "I like it; it's cool—honestly." Brody brightened. Shaking his hand, the girl introduced herself: "Welcome! My name is Fatima. Fatima Talkie."

"Well, it's nice to meet you, Fatima," Brody said, tipping an imaginary hat. Fatima stared at him confusedly. *Note to self*, Brody thought, *never do that again.*

"So, did I hear you say you're in first-period chemistry?" Fatima asked. Brody nodded. "Awesome, me too!" Fatima said. "I'm heading that way now, if you want to walk with me."

"Totally!" Brody replied, smiling. *I made a friend.* It felt a little silly to be proud of that, but on the first day in a new school (especially here), it seemed like a big accomplishment. On the way to chemistry, he learned more about Fatima Talkie (who, Brody discovered, loved to talk): She had been born and raised in Washington, DC, and was also in the seventh grade. She had two dogs, a cat, and three brothers. ("Ranked in that order," she told Brody.) And, to Brody's surprise, she loved the outdoors—just like him! They immediately started talking about their favorite hiking spots and trails. "We should go on a hike sometime," Fatima said.

In chemistry, Mrs. Tuff paired Brody and Fatima together as lab partners. ("Yeehaw!" Brody exclaimed in celebration. Fatima laughed.) Less fortunately, the class itself was a disaster. *Why is the material so confusing?* Brody thought. At the end of class, Mrs. Tuff handed out a homework assignment. Looking at it, Brody felt panicked. *Neutrons? What are neutrons?* His classes here seemed much more advanced than anything he'd done in Louisville. "Do you know what any of this stuff is?" he whispered to Fatima.

She rolled her eyes. "Nope . . . not really. They make it

super hard on purpose. But we'll figure it out! Here, give me your number. We can check our answers later tonight." A second later, she'd texted Brody:

> It's Fatima T.!

And then, "Oh! And are you on SocialBook?"

"Yeah!" Brody said. "I'm @Brody McCool Kid." A second later, another notification popped up on his phone. @Fatima the titan has requested to follow you. The bell rang.

"Well, I'm off to Spanish!" Fatima said. "But I'll see you tomorrow, Brody!" Brody waved as she walked off.

That definitely could've been worse, Brody thought. *Maybe this place won't be so terrible after all.*

⚠ #️⃣

Riiiiiiing! As soon as she heard the final bell ring, Fatima Talkie walked out of eighth-period English and boarded school bus #9. "Hello there, Ms. Talkie!" the bus driver, Mrs. Galpal, said. Mrs. Galpal had been driving Fatima to school since kindergarten. "How was the first day? I need my status update!"

"I'll have a full report for you later, Mrs. Galpal, but not bad!" Fatima replied, returning her high five. And that was the truth—it hadn't been that bad. Her Spanish teacher, Señor Simpatico, seemed really nice, and pre-algebra was going to be a piece of cake. Of course, chemistry had been a little tricky, but she'd made a new friend, which definitely made it better. *What was his name again? Brady? Oh, wait!* "Brody," Fatima said to herself thoughtfully. *Brody McNewKid.* She liked him. *Maybe this year won't be a bust*, she thought.

Fatima was still in a good mood when she arrived home. She headed to the kitchen to grab a snack—but immediately stopped dead in her tracks. There, at the table, were her parents. By the looks of it, they were waiting for her, and they didn't seem happy. Her dad looked solemn, and her mom's eyes were red. *Uh-oh*, Fatima thought. *They want to talk.* Whenever her parents wanted "to talk," it was never good; the last time she'd found them like this, they'd told her Aunt Laila had passed away. "Hey," Fatima said, her voice wavering, betraying her nervousness.

"Hey, sweetie," her dad said. "How was your first day?"

"Pretty good," Fatima said cautiously. She hated small talk. "So . . . what's going on?"

"Why don't you sit?" her mom said, pulling out a chair. Fatima sighed. *Here we go.*

The next hour was a blur. Her parents talked on and on, endlessly, it seemed, but Fatima had stopped listening after her dad dropped the bombshell: "Your mother and I are getting a divorce."

Fatima felt like she'd had the wind knocked out of her. *A divorce?* She couldn't imagine a world where her parents weren't together. *How can this be happening?* "Am I going to have to choose one of you?" she'd cried out. Immediately, her parents had started another round of reassurances—nothing

35

was going to change, really; her dad was going to move out, but they both loved her so much, and she'd continue to see him regularly . . .

I can't be the only one who thinks this is a terrible idea, Fatima thought bitterly. Which reminded her—her brothers! "What about Hamza, Faizan, and Ali?" she asked suddenly. "Do they know?"

Her parents looked at each other. "Yes, actually; we told them last night," her mom said apprehensively. *What?! They told them before me?* She opened her mouth in protest, but her dad quickly interjected: "We didn't want to ruin your first day."

"And this is better?" Fatima asked.

Her dad looked at the floor. "We know you're disappointed," he said. "But in the long run, we think this is going to be better for everyone—including you."

Fatima felt her anger boil over. *How do they know what would be good for me? And how could they do this to me?* "The only people you did this for are you two!" she yelled, tears rolling down her face.

Her mom reached out as if to touch her, but Fatima slapped her hand away. Her mom recoiled, shocked. "Fatima Talkie! We know that this is a lot, but that was incredibly inappropriate," she said. "You need to apologize now."

Fatima smirked. "Oh yeah? Here's your apology: I hate you." Turning her back on them, Fatima ran out of the kitchen and up to her room. There, she began to sob. It felt as if her whole world was crumbling.

Buzz. Fatima jumped at the sound of her phone. Wiping her eyes, she grabbed it. *Who is texting?* "Oh," she said to herself. "Brody McNewKid." The message read:

> Hey! Let me know when u finish the chemistry hw! We can chk answrs.

A second later, another message appeared. Fatima squinted. *Is that a picture?* She clicked on it. It was Brody, surrounded by a bunch of people—his parents and siblings, it looked like—on the top of a cliff. *Buzz.* Another text from Brody:

> Thought u would like this—my family after a hike on Whitethorpe Mountain! I know u said ur dad likes Whitethorpe.

At the mention of her dad, Fatima bristled. *I'll never go on a hike with my family again*, she realized sadly. "And it's all because of my idiotic parents," she said angrily, out loud this time.

Buzz. "Oh my god!" Fatima exclaimed in frustration. She grabbed her phone. "Who's texting *now*?" It was Brody—again!

> Here's another 1: Chicopee Mountain.

Below the text was another picture of Brody's family.

Fatima was enraged. Why did he keep sending her these pictures? She didn't want to see pictures of his dumb family! Before she knew it, she was typing:

> Do me a favor and GO AWAY. I don't want to talk to you, and I don't care about your stupid family.

Whoosh. She'd sent the message. Reading it back, Fatima felt a little surprised at herself, but she also felt a moment of satisfaction. *Take that, McNewKid. He's so annoying.*

To distract herself, Fatima switched over to SocialBook. Usually, her parents had a strict time limit rule, but she doubted they'd be enforcing it tonight. *Might as well take the good with the bad*, Fatima thought bitterly. She scrolled through the pictures, and for a few minutes, everything felt normal: Tamika Melody had posted a picture of her new guitar ("So rad!" Fatima commented), and Jordan Beacher was sharing pictures of his summer on Cape Cod. But then . . . Fatima did a double take. *Who's that? Oh . . . it's a post from Brody.*

@BRODYMCCOOLKID: **I got my family, my dog, and my boots—all I need up in Washington D.C.! #FirstDay.** He'd shared several photos, including one of the boots he'd been wearing that day, one of his dog—a labradoodle, it seemed—and one of him and his parents, flanking him and smiling brightly.

Of course, Fatima thought, exasperated. *Leave it to Brody McLoser to rub his family in my face.* Staring at the picture,

Fatima felt a rush of anger and pain, and suddenly, she was typing out a comment: "Friendly piece of fashion advice: leave the boots at home. NO ONE likes them!" She quickly hit POST and exhaled.

A second later, a notification appeared on her phone. *Ping!* @JIMNASTIE LIKED YOUR COMMENT! And then another: @DJHATEFOL LIKED YOUR COMMENT! Her comment was blowing up. Fatima felt bad, but then she remembered: he'd hurt her first. *But he didn't mean to*, a voice in the back of her head said. Fatima pushed the thought away. She was sick of Brody McNewKid and his perfect family. *And this is payback.*

Buzz. Fatima peered down at her phone. *Uh-oh.* Brody had texted her:

> Hey. Did I do something? Y are u mad at me?

Then, a minute later, another message:

> Tht comment on SocialBook was not cool. What is going on?

Great, Fatima thought. *I can't do this right now.* She threw her phone across the room and curled up in the middle of her bed. She could still hear her phone pinging as person after person liked her comment on SocialBook. "At least you're not the only one having a bad night," she whispered to herself before closing her eyes.

39

Across town, lying in his bed, Brody McNewKid couldn't sleep. He was still struggling to wrap his head around what had happened with Fatima. *It seemed like she liked me*, Brody thought. *I thought we were starting to be friends.* He sighed and turned over, pulling the covers up. *Maybe I said something, or did something. Or maybe . . .* He squeezed his eyes shut, trying to avoid the thought that'd been bothering him all evening. *Maybe the whole thing—her offer of friendship, being nice—was a prank. Maybe I bought into a lie.* The thought made Brody cringe, and a wave of shame and embarrassment overcame him. *I'm such a loser*, he thought. *But on the other hand . . . she seemed so sincere.* Maybe the kids in Washington, DC, were better actors than they were in Louisville. (Brody certainly wouldn't have been surprised.)

He glanced at the clock next to his bed—three a.m.—and groaned. *Great—tomorrow, I'll fall asleep in homeroom, and Mr. Stricter will give me detention.* Staring out the window, he'd never felt so alone. "I just want to go home," he whispered quietly. He knew it made him sound lame, but it was the truth. He was done with Fatima Talkie, and he was *so* done with Washington, DC.

Tired of tossing and turning, Brody figured he'd head downstairs and warm up a mug of milk. *Maybe that'll do the trick.* As he descended the stairs, he was surprised to see the light in the kitchen was on. *What?* Peeking his head in, he saw his older sister, Sarah, sitting at the counter—sipping milk! *It's not just me*, Brody thought, his heart warming.

"Hey there, BroKid," Sarah said, ruffling his hair. Brody

hated her nickname for him, but at that moment, it felt familiar and welcoming. "What are you doing down here?" she asked.

"I could ask the same of you," Brody replied in turn. "What are you doing down here?"

"Whoa, whoa, whoa . . . I was here first," Sarah said, putting her hands up in mock indignation. "My kitchen, my rules. *You* have to answer first."

"Um . . ." Brody was at a loss. *Where to begin?* He opened his mouth to explain but let out a sob; a second later, he was crying. With Sarah hugging and patting him, he explained everything that had happened at school—from homeroom with Mr. Stricter, to his insanely difficult chemistry class with Mrs. Tuff, to the Fatima Talkie debacle. "And so . . . I have no idea what happened, or what to do about it. All I know is I'm a complete loser, I have no friends, and I hate this place." Finished, he felt a sense of shame settle on him. *Crying to Sarah, McNewKid?* he thought. *How humiliating.* Would this night ever end?

Sarah hugged him tightly. "I'm glad you came to me, Brody," she said gently. "Trust me, it hasn't been easy on any of us—even Mom and Dad. And I— I'm struggling to make friends too. It's just all so different," she said with a sigh. "But you have to take it one step at a time, or it'll be too much." She straightened up. "So start with Fatima—try and fix whatever went wrong there."

"C'mon!" Brody moaned. "Why do *I* have to fix it? I didn't do anything wrong; she did!"

"True," Sarah said thoughtfully. "But, if I were to guess, something probably happened to Fatima—maybe something difficult or awful—and she's taking it out on you." Brody started. *Could that be it?* "Of course, what she did wasn't right, and she needs to apologize," Sarah said. "But sometimes, people need our forgiveness when they least deserve it. And if you want to make a friend . . . well, there's no better way."

Sarah's right, Brody realized. *I need to talk to Fatima.* He hugged his sister tightly. "Thank you, Sarah." Maybe his sister wasn't so bad after all.

The next morning, Fatima Talkie stared at herself in her locker mirror in horror. *I look like a zombie.* She'd forgotten to set her alarm, so when she awoke, she was already late; she'd randomly grabbed a sweater and a pair of pants from her drawer and had run out the door to catch the school bus. She hadn't even brushed her teeth! And her hair . . . She hadn't brushed it, either, so it looked like there were two mops—one purple, the other green—on either side of her head. Fatima sighed and looked down—*Crud!* Sitting there in her locker was her chemistry homework—which she had forgotten to complete. And speaking of chemistry homework . . . there was the matter of seeing Brody McAnnoying in chemistry. *This day sucks*, Fatima thought. *All thanks to Mom and Dad.* They weren't speaking to her—not until she apologized, supposedly—as if she'd done something wrong! *They're never getting an apology.*

"Hey . . . uh . . . Fatima?" *Oh no. That voice sounds very familiar . . . It can't be . . .*

Fatima swung around. It was Brody! *What is he doing here? Did he not get the message?* Crossing his arms, he met her stare evenly. "Can I talk to you for a second?" he asked. Fatima nodded, suddenly nervous.

Brody let out a deep sigh. "Fatima . . . why would you ever send me that text? Or post that comment?" he asked, his face pained. "I have absolutely no idea what I did . . . or if something happened."

Fatima felt herself deflate. Looking at him now, she felt a lot less brave than she had on her phone the day before.

"You really hurt me, Fatima," Brody continued. "I just . . . want to know why."

Suddenly, Fatima was flooded with guilt—she knew she never should've said what she had, but she'd been so angry. *Yeah, because he kept sending those pictures!* "Why did you have to send me those pictures?" she asked, frustrated. Brody looked confused. "Of your family!" Fatima exclaimed. "Why would you think I care?"

"I thought you liked hiking!" Brody said. "Besides, it's just a picture! Why do you hate my family so much?"

"Because I don't have one!" Fatima hollered. *Wait. Did I just say that out loud?* Around her, she could sense other students staring, then turning to one another and whispering. Her cheeks warming, she looked down. *This is so humiliating.*

She waited for Brody's retort, but it never came. Looking up, she saw he looked concerned. *He wants to help, Fatima,* the voice in the back of her head said. *And he didn't know.* She sighed. "Yesterday after school, my parents told me they're getting a divorce," she muttered, and felt tears collecting in her eyes.

"Hey, hey, hey," Brody said. Before she knew it, he was hugging her. *What?* "I'm really sorry," he said. *Why is he apologizing?* "That sucks. I'm sure it's been tough to deal with."

In that moment, Fatima realized—she had become one of the jerks at Newbie she so despised! She'd let her feelings get the better of her—and it'd been so easy on her phone. Now she felt terrible . . . and she couldn't believe what she'd done to Brody. *And in spite of it all, he's still being nice to me.* "Brody . . ." She took a deep breath. "I'm so, so sorry," she said, shaking her head. "I was really mad, and I wasn't thinking—and it was sort of easy to be a jerk, you know? I totally get it if you don't want to talk to me again." Nervously, she looked up at Brody.

"It's okay," Brody said, nodding. "I get it. Mistakes happen, and no one's perfect." He smiled at her. "Why don't we just put it behind us?" Fatima nodded.

"So . . ." Brody glanced at her locker. "Do you need help with the chemistry homework?" he asked, raising his eyebrows. A second later, they both burst out laughing. As she pulled out the homework, Fatima felt herself relax. *It's all going to be okay*, she realized. *And that truly is enough.*

CHAPTER 2 INTERNET CHALLENGE

Congratulations on completing chapter 2! You've learned one of the most important internet lessons out there: **internet people are real people too.**

Whether moving to a new town and joining a new school, encountering a life-changing event, or dealing with some pretty tough chemistry homework, Brody and Fatima's story is one you may have some experience with. As we saw in Fatima's case, turning to her phone to deal with her troubles was *not* the answer. Later, she had to face the consequences—a tough conversation, and that awful feeling when you know you're in the wrong. If she had remembered our mantra—**if you wouldn't say it to someone's face, don't say it online**—she might have avoided all of that trouble. Sometimes, though, we all make mistakes—a fact that Brody's sister, Sarah, was quick to recognize. Rather than "getting his own revenge" or fighting fire with fire, Brody offered Fatima forgiveness and ensured that a bad situation didn't become worse.

Now that you've read Brody and Fatima's story, it's time for you to get your internet expertise on! For this Internet Challenge, the next time you're about to say something questionable online, ask yourself: *Would I say this to someone's face?* Then, remind yourself—and the world—that internet people are real people too by sharing a post of the most important people in your life. Whether it's a picture with a family member at Christmas or one of your best friends, make sure to use the hashtag "#InternetPositivity."

Trisha's post:

@TrishPrabhu: My dad and I are really excited to enjoy some deep dish on my birthday #20! 😋🍕 Sending a little #InternetPositivity to the best dad for making this birthday so special, love you 🖤

CHAPTER 3
IT'S NOT ALWAYS TRUE?!

When you don't know something, what do you do? Head to the library? Nah. You look it up on the internet, of course! And it's true—the internet is a great resource for expanding your knowledge; it's filled to the brim with information! There's so much floating around out there—websites, news, images, videos, and more. And all of it—all of the information, written and delivered by so many people—can make it seem like the internet is the last word on anything you can imagine. I hate to break the news, but . . . spoiler alert: that's not always true! With so much information out there, it's hard to check and see if every last bit and piece is actually right. There's no official "internet police" hunting down the folks who spread—whether purposely or accidentally—inaccurate information. In fact, the issue is so common that we have fancy terms for unreliable information: when it's spread on purpose, it's called "disinformation"; when it's accidental, it's called "misinformation." TL;DR: it's important, then, not to trust everything you see or read online. The internet has fooled some of the best of us—including me (as it turns out, chocolate isn't a "misunderstood" vegetable . . . Oops 😆). Don't let it fool you!

Be a Digital Detective

But how, Trisha?! you might be wondering. *How do I filter through everything I see online?* Here's a list of "digital detective" tips I use to ensure that the internet can't trick me! In just four steps, you can get ahead of all of that information. Warning: These tips might make you an internet superhero.

1. First up: Check the source! Is this a company's website, or your uncle's blog? If it's the latter, you should be skeptical of the information you're reading (after all, there's no telling what your uncle might say)! Established institutions and organizations, such as government agencies, are much, much more trustworthy than a random person's blog. TL;DR: .org > .com.

2. Check the date! When was this article/page/media/piece of information written or shared? If it was a few months ago, it's probably still applicable. If it was a few years ago, that might be less true. You wouldn't trust an article that says the Jonas Brothers are fifteen, fourteen, and thirteen, right?

3. Avoid anonymity. If you're not sure who wrote the article,

or a name isn't listed, it probably isn't worth your time. If someone isn't willing to own the information they share, it's unlikely that that information is reputable, or trustworthy.

4. Check for bias! I still remember the time my mom tried to sell me on singing at our family Christmas party (I have two words for you: so embarrassing). She thinks I have a "divine" singing voice. The truth? I do not, but she's biased . . . because she's my mom! Of course, she made it sound like I was a budding Beyoncé ("Any record label would sign you!") . . . which is why I should've known, right then and there, that it would be the worst. The same concept applies online. If you see language that seems just a little too extreme, beware. The author may have an agenda—and potentially one more nefarious than my mom's!

Now that you have the insider info, let's head on over to our story!

Breathing deeply, Sherlock Solver took a step back from his desk. *Concentrate, Sherlock*, he willed himself. He'd put in hours and hours of hard work to finally reach this moment— he couldn't afford to mess it up now. *Where's the connection? Find the connection.* He stared down at his desk, his eyes scanning the setup. In front of him, papers, figures, and various objects lay across his desk. The documents were a mess—words had been underlined and circled, and stray notes dotted the margins—and several of the objects were chipped and peeling, but none of that mattered. All that mattered was the line of multicolored yarn Sherlock had strung along from document to document: it was there, intertwined in the red, white, and blue (he'd found the yarn in his dad's shed, left over from the family's Fourth of July celebrations) that the answer to his mystery lay. *Wait.* He looked back at the first document on his desk. *Aha. There it is—four p.m.* He looked across the desk at another document. *Bingo! The Musickers leave for music lessons every Saturday at four p.m.* He was so close; now all he needed was a motive. He could practically smell the possibility. "Victory . . . will soon be—"

Meow! Sherlock looked up, startled. The family cat, Ginger, sprang into his room. She deftly climbed his desk and pounced on top of the display, swiping excitedly at the yarn. "Ginger, no!" Sherlock yelled, furious. "Get away from there, now!" Before he could grab her, she pranced off his desk, heading for his older brother's room—but the damage was done. The documents were now all over his bedroom floor, and his carefully placed line was in ruins. "Argh!" Sherlock yelled, throwing his hands up in frustration. *Another mystery foiled!*

There was a knock at the door. His mom peeked in. "Honey, what are you doing there?"

"Nothing, Mom," Sherlock said as he tried to block her view of the mess—but it was too late.

"That didn't sound like nothing to me . . ." his mom said,

stepping into his room. Her eyes widened. "Oh my good-ness, Sherlock! What on earth is all of this?" Behind her, Sherlock's older brother appeared. Staring at the mess, he began to laugh. *Argh*, Sherlock thought. *Leave it to Mom to help Ken humiliate me.*

"Hello? Is anyone at home?" His mom tapped her fingers loudly on Sherlock's desk, jolting him out of his thoughts. "Sherlock Solver, you answer me this minute!"

"It was just a little mystery work, Mom!" Sherlock said, an-noyed. "This is a really big case! And I was so close to cracking it . . . until Ginger came along." He shook his head and sighed.

"What was the mystery, little bro?" Ken asked, his smile widening. "Another nerdy case that no one cares about?"

Sherlock rolled his eyes. "Why would I tell you? It's not like you'd be able to help . . . You have the IQ of a fruit fly!" he retorted.

Ken started, as if to grab him, but his mom interjected. "No! Just this one time, no fighting!" Ken's eyes narrowed, displeased. *Ha*, Sherlock thought. *Serves him right.*

"Hold on," his mom said. Sherlock looked up at her. She was staring at the floor. "Is that . . . a picture of Mrs. Musicker? Our neighbor?"

Is this ever going to end? Exasperated, Sherlock sighed again, this time more deeply. "It's clear that none of you re-call, but five days ago, at approximately 4:03 p.m., the Solver family baseball disappeared from the backyard. While it may not have had a ton of financial value, it did mean a lot to all of us, which means whoever took the ball has a serious grudge against our family." His mom and Ken looked at each other, and then at him, alarmed. *Finally*, Sherlock thought. *An interested audience.* "Now, over the past seventy-two hours, I have compiled all of the relevant evidence—and I have reason to believe that it was the Musickers. I have yet to determine the motive, but in time—"

Sherlock's narration was interrupted by Ken. He collapsed to the floor in laughter, holding the sides of his stomach. "You . . . think . . . it . . . was . . . the . . . Musickers?" he asked, breathing heavily. "Dude, it was Ginger! Ginger grabbed the ball! It's downstairs, with all of her toys!"

What?! Sherlock was aghast. *That can't be true . . .* Pushing past his mom, he ran to the kitchen. Nestled behind Ginger's water bowl, along with all of her toys, was . . . the baseball; Sherlock could see SOLVER etched on its side. Staring at the floor, Sherlock could feel his face burning. *I spent three days solving a mystery that didn't exist*, he realized.

He felt a hand on his shoulder. It was his mom. She smiled softly and kissed his cheek (as Sherlock did his best to get away). "It was a good effort, honey," she said gently. "One day, you'll find your breakthrough mystery. It just takes time!"

Sherlock nodded wordlessly—he was still in a state of shock (and mortification). "You know what will make you feel better?" his mom asked. Sherlock shook his head. "Lunch!" she said brightly. "I made soybean sprouts soup!"

Ewwww. Sherlock wrinkled his nose. "Soybeans?! Mom, you know I hate that stuff!"

"C'mon! Just try it," his mom said as she placed the bowl

of soup in front of him. "It's a family recipe, all the way from Korea."

Sherlock groaned. "Fine," he said.

As Sherlock tentatively dipped his spoon into the soup, his mom grabbed her phone and settled onto the couch. A minute later, she squealed. Sherlock looked up, confused, as his mom walked over, seemingly thrilled. "Sherlock! Guess what I just saw on SocialGram?" She was so excited, she was practically bouncing up and down.

"What?" Sherlock asked in monotone.

His mom swatted him in mock indignation. "You'll want to hear this!" Lowering her voice, she whispered across the table, "Dustin Dieber's favorite dish is soybean soup! You're eating food of the gods!"

Sherlock grimaced. *Oh dear.* His mom's favorite singer— and forever celebrity crush—was Dustin Dieber. Whenever Dustin did anything, it was good enough for his mom; earlier that year, she'd made the entire family go to a goat yoga session after she'd read it was "Dustin's favorite hobby." *This guy doesn't know it, but he's ruining people's lives*, Sherlock thought darkly. "Wow, Mom," he said unenthusiastically. "That's . . . so cool."

His mom didn't notice his tone. "I know! I saw it on diebergossip.com! I'm going to share it on my SocialGram page right now."

As his mom busied herself with her phone, Sherlock looked down at his soup. *This day went downhill fast*, he thought.

The next day, Sherlock was still in a bad mood over the base-ball case. He moped around the house, finally settling on the couch in his living room, idly flipping through shows on TV. He'd hoped the case would be a reprieve from what had been an uncharacteristically boring summer, but instead, he'd made a fool of himself. And in front of his brother! *I'll never live it down*, he thought angrily. Usually, summer was Sherlock's favorite time of the year: no school, and no homework—just time to sleep, play video games, and hang out with his two best friends, Isaiah Imallergic and Marty Tuba. This summer, though, things hadn't quite worked out that way: Marty had decided to go to band camp all the way in Chicago, and after his parents had gotten a divorce earlier that year, Isaiah was spending the summer with his dad in the Hamptons. So it was just Sherlock . . . and his family. Thus far, that had meant Ken "borrowing" his video games without asking, his mom force-feeding him Dustin Dieber's supposed favorite foods, and his dad telling him to "end all of this mystery business now. You're thirteen, Sherlock! It's time to get serious." About what, he'd never said.

I wish I could prove him wrong, Sherlock thought. More than anything, that was what he wanted: to crack a big case before the start of the school year. He could see it now: the local police department would anoint him with an honor-ary "junior detective" badge at a fancy ceremony—as his dad smiled proudly, his mom livestreamed the event to

SocialGram, and even Ken admitted Sherlock was "pretty cool." *Then, when the year starts, everyone at school will love me . . . maybe even Zara Dreamgirl.* Sherlock smiled goofily at the thought.

Buzz. Sherlock's phone interrupted his reverie. Annoyed, Sherlock grabbed it. *Of course,* he thought. *The universe couldn't let me be happy for more than five seconds. Except . . .*

He'd received a text from Isaiah!

> Hey man! Just got back from my dad's. Wanna hang out?

Sherlock's spirits lifted. *Isaiah is back! Maybe this summer can be salvaged!* He quickly typed back:

> Yes dude. My house?

A second later, Isaiah had responded:

Finally! His misery had come to a close. *The summer is back on track.*

"Sherlock!" he heard his mom call out. Inwardly, Sherlock groaned. "I'm about to make lunch—do you want some kimchi? Or chicken parmesan?" She walked into the living room. "They're both Dustin Dieber favorites!" She smiled gleefully.

Sherlock sighed, and then remembered—*Isaiah.* "Actually, Mom, Isaiah is coming over . . . and I think he has a wheat sensitivity. It's not serious or anything, but I know he tries to avoid certain foods. So maybe something without wheat?"

"Ah yes," his mom said. "Let me see, now . . ." She grabbed her phone. "There's a great blog I use for all things food," she explained. "*Dr. Rong's Food Encyclopedia!* He has over five thousand posts on all sorts of different cuisines; he's practically an expert . . ." She scrolled furiously on her phone. "Let's see, now . . . *C, C, C,* here we go—chicken parmesan! Allergens: no wheat," she announced. "And Dr. Rong's never wrong! I think I'll do the chicken parmesan, then. Does that sound good, Sherlock?"

Sherlock jumped; he'd stopped listening as soon as she'd reached for her phone. *No need to get the lowdown on another Dustin Dieber trend!* "Sounds great, Mom," he said, nodding absently. His mom clapped her hands and walked into the kitchen. *I don't really care what she makes for lunch,* Sherlock thought. *Isaiah is back!*

When Isaiah arrived, they immediately headed up to Sherlock's game room. Before long, they were playing the new game Sherlock had bought recently—*Mystery Mansion 2.0*—and chowing on the wheat-free brownies Isaiah brought with him—their all-time favorite snack. Isaiah told Sherlock all about the Hamptons: "It was fun, but I really missed home, and my dad's a terrible chef." And Sherlock told him all about the Solver baseball mystery fiasco. "I need to crack a case soon, dude," he said, sighing. "Otherwise, my dad's never going to let me do mystery work . . . and I'll end up doing something totally lame."

"Like what?" Isaiah asked.

Sherlock considered. "Like . . . being an accountant," he said, his eyes widening in horror. "What do they even do?"

Isaiah shook his head and shivered. "I dunno, and I don't want to find out. You're right, man. We need to fix this situation ASAP."

Sherlock sighed. Isaiah patted him on the back. "Don't sweat it, bro. We'll figure it out! I'll help you find a case." Sherlock brightened. "I can be like . . . an assistant detective or something," Isaiah said.

Sherlock smiled. *I'm back in the game. With Isaiah's help, I'll find a case, and then glory will actually be mine . . .*

"Boys?" Sherlock heard his mom's voice. "Lunch is ready! Come and get it!"

Isaiah set his game console down. "*Yes!* I'm starving . . . for anything my dad hasn't made." They raced down the stairs to the kitchen.

Sherlock immediately took his seat at the table and served himself a generous helping of chicken parmesan. His stomach grumbled; he'd been so preoccupied with his failed mystery, he'd forgotten how hungry he was! It was only mid-bite that he realized Isaiah was still standing at the door, looking at the table, his face uncertain.

57

"Uh . . . dude?" Sherlock asked, confused. Isaiah had the biggest appetite of any of his friends. "What are you doing? You don't have to be polite. Just grab some food, like always!"

"I don't think I can," Isaiah said, hesitating. "Doesn't chicken parmesan have wheat in it?" Sherlock looked over at his mom.

"Well, you're in luck, because this recipe is wheat-free!" Sherlock's mom trilled. Isaiah looked relieved. "I found it on a very reputable website; rest assured that the chef, Dr. Rong, is never wrong. He has so many fans; it's impossible that he could be! Let me check again," she said, grabbing her phone. "Yes—it says right here: no wheat. Of course, I'm happy to make you something else, if you'd prefer."

Isaiah shook his head. "In that case, this looks great! Thank you, Mrs. S!" He grabbed a plate and dug in.

"You know, Sherlock," his mom said, joining them at the table. "I've been thinking—I might require your help with a little mystery work."

Sherlock looked up, astonished. *A case? I didn't think I'd get one so easily!* He looked over at Isaiah excitedly, but Isaiah didn't seem to be paying any attention. When he finally caught his eye— *Was that a grimace? Weird.* He turned to his mom. "So . . . what's the case?"

His mom sighed dramatically. "Unfortunately, it seems that Dustin Dieber has gone missing. No one on SocialGram has seen him for forty-eight hours!" she exclaimed, wringing her hands. *Argh*, Sherlock thought. *Not him!* "Uh, Mom . . . I'm not really a Dustin Dieber kind of detective."

His mom looked indignant. "Why not? The man is a treasure!"

Think of something, Sherlock thought. "Well . . . uh . . . different detectives have different specialties, you know? And mine . . . mine is not people . . . like Dustin. So that's why I can't help . . . right, Isaiah?"

Sherlock turned to his friend for backup. *Wait*. "Isaiah?!"

In unison, he and his mom gasped. Isaiah's face was all red and blotchy, and he seemed to have broken out in hives. He was scratching his arms, and when he spoke, his voice was hoarse: "I think . . . the chicken . . . parmesan . . . had wheat in it," he said, his words punctuated by coughing. Sherlock's mom immediately ran to the medicine cabinet, and she poured out some anti-allergy syrup. After taking it, Isaiah seemed to be a bit better . . . but was still scratching his body vigorously.

Looking at him, Sherlock felt very bad for his friend—but there was another part of him, just a small part, that was excited. He knew this wasn't how Isaiah had intended to help him, but nevertheless, he now had a new mystery to solve: Who'd added wheat to the chicken parmesan? *The recipe was wheat-free*, Sherlock reasoned, *which means it had to have been an external source. Maybe a nemesis from band camp, or even Ken, trying to play a prank!* No matter what, he resolved, he'd get to the bottom of this.

Sherlock's mom was aghast. "I . . . I . . . just don't know how this happened!" she stuttered. "In any case, that's not what matters right now . . . Isaiah, how are you feeling?"

Isaiah looked worried. "Honestly, not great. The last time this happened, my mom took me to the doctor," he said.

Now Sherlock's mom looked worried too. "Then that's where we should go. Sherlock, go grab my keys! I'll let Isaiah's mom know what happened, and to meet us there."

"Okay, Mom!" Sherlock said. *I'll also make a quick pit stop in my room*, he thought. *I'm going to need a notebook to record everything the doctor says. Sherlock Solver is back on the case!*

"Open your mouth," Dr. Truthteller instructed. "Hmmm . . ." he mused as he examined Isaiah's throat. "Well . . . it's not that bad, but you're definitely going to take some meds for the rest of the week." As if to emphasize his point, a second later, Isaiah started coughing; Sherlock's mom patted him on the back, her face concerned.

Sherlock looked up from his notes. "Dr. Truthteller, if I may?" he asked, standing up. Dr. Truthteller looked at him over his glasses, his face curious. "Yes, Sherlock?"

Sherlock cleared his throat. *Showtime.* "Given the evidence, I have reason to believe that we need to file a police report." Dr. Truthteller's eyes widened. "Based on your assessment, it's clear that the allergic reaction was a result of the chicken parmesan, but we know that the meal was wheat-free. So an external actor—malicious, clearly—must've planted a wheat-based substance in the chicken parmesan." Dr. Truthteller stood up, as if to interrupt him, but Sherlock interjected. "Hold on—I'm not done yet. I know what you're thinking: Who could have done this? I've yet to determine who, exactly, had access to the kitchen, but right now, my primary suspect is Ken Solver, my brother. He's a prankster who, if history is reliable, probably had nothing else to do." *That will teach Ken not to mess with my friends . . . He's gone way too far this time!*

"Sherlock Solver!" His mom stood up, furious. "What on earth do you think you're doing?"

"Mrs. Solver, I think I can handle this one," Dr. Truthteller said, turning to Sherlock. Smiling, he shook his head. "Good detective work, Sherlock; I'm very impressed. Unfortunately, I'm not quite sure that Ken is responsible. In fact, the vast majority of chicken parmesan recipes have wheat." He glanced over at Sherlock's mom. "I'm not sure what recipe you were looking at, Mrs. Solver, but I wouldn't consult that source again."

"It's a highly reputable source, Dr. Truthteller!" Sherlock's mom exclaimed, indignant. She consulted her phone. "*Dr. Rong's Food Encyclopedia* has over ten million followers on SocialGram alone. And will you look at how handsome he is?" Hands on her hips, she looked at Dr. Truthteller. "Are you saying he lied to his readers? I find that hard to believe," she said, shaking her head.

"Not at all, Mrs. Solver," Dr. Truthteller said diplomatically. "I've heard of Dr. Rong, and while I'm sure he's very popular—and even handsome—I also know he isn't actually a doctor. He uses the title to boost his credibility, so folks will spend more time on his website." *What?* Sherlock was shocked. All along, he'd been mired in one mystery . . . when there'd been another one right in front of him! "That's not to say that this was malicious. It's entirely possible that he accidentally mislabeled the recipe 'wheat-free,'" Dr. Truthteller continued. "In any case, you're a lot less likely to run into those kinds of errors on better sites. I'd highly recommend food.gov."

Sherlock's mom was stunned. "I can't believe this," she said sadly. "I really trusted him . . . but I guess . . . I was wrong." Sherlock couldn't believe it, either: he'd never thought it was possible that his mom would be wrong about something! *I always believe everything she says* . . . Suddenly, the world seemed a lot less certain to Sherlock.

Dr. Truthteller patted her gently. "It happens to the best of us! Now you know, for the future."

As Dr. Truthteller headed out, Mrs. Imallergic ran in. "Oh, Isaiah! You're okay!" she exclaimed, hugging him.

"Get off me, Mom," he complained.

Both moms started to chat, shaking their heads. "I'm so sorry, Helen," Mrs. Solver said. "I had no idea!"

Sherlock walked over to where Isaiah was sitting. "I'm really sorry, dude," Sherlock said. He'd been so wrapped up in the supposed mystery, he'd forgotten the ordeal his best friend had just been through—and he felt horrible. "Feel better . . . and when you do, text me. We still need to beat the next level of *Mystery Mansion!*"

Isaiah smiled weakly. "Definitely, dude. And . . . truly, it's no one's fault. Besides, as my mom will definitely tell me, I should've known better." A few minutes later, he left with his mom, and Sherlock and Mrs. Solver silently headed home.

Back in his room, Sherlock couldn't stop pacing restlessly. He was still absorbing the afternoon's revelations . . . and Isaiah's comment that he "should've known better." *Isaiah was right*, Sherlock realized. When Sherlock solved mysteries, he generally assumed the facts he had were right. Most of those facts came from adults, and adults were always right . . . Right? *But what if they aren't? . . . Then those are the biggest traps around*, Sherlock realized. *If the internet can fool Mom, it can definitely fool me.* He wasn't going to forget that; grabbing his notebook, he quickly scribbled an entry: "July 25th: lesson of the day—keep an eye out for lies!"

Later that evening, Sherlock joined his family at the dinner table. *Leftover chicken parmesan. Ha*, Sherlock thought. *Ah, the irony.* Across the table, his mom, usually chatty, was silent. Sherlock could tell she was still unhappy about the afternoon's events. He felt a pang of sympathy— *We were all tricked by Dr. Rong's website.* He knew how to cheer her up, but he also knew he was going to regret it . . . *Eh . . . here goes*, he thought. "So, Mom . . . have you heard anything about

Dustin Dieber? Were they finally able to find him?" he asked. His dad and Ken looked up at him, their faces surprised. Ken stared at him, his eyes piercing, as if to say: *Why would you say the D word?*

Rather than squeal in excitement, Sherlock's mom sighed. "No . . . All of my SocialGram information sources say that the authorities are trying to find him, but there's no sign of him."

Great, Sherlock thought. *That really backfired.* In any case, the detective in him was intrigued. *Could this be a mystery to solve? Yes, it was about Dustin Dieber, but seeing as he didn't have any others . . .* He spent the rest of dinner questioning his mom about the case, making careful notes on his notepad. (Next to them, his dad and Ken glared. *Whatever.*)

Back in his room, Sherlock rummaged around in his "detective drawer," as he called it, until he found what he was looking for— *There it is. My ball of yarn!* On his desk, he carefully began to set up the case, just as he had when he'd been investigating the missing Solver baseball. When he was finished, he checked back against his notes. *Did I miss anything?* He noticed his entry from earlier that evening: "July 25th: lesson of the day—keep an eye out for lies!"

Hold on. Sherlock's eyes widened. *Could it be . . . ?* He dashed to his laptop and quickly typed out a search: "Dustin Dieber missing." A list of results appeared—all SocialGram pages with tributes to Dustin. **Come back soon, buddy,** one caption read, with the hashtags **#PrayForDustin** and **#WeLoveYouDustin.**

Hmm . . . the disappearance seems legit. Still, after everything that had happened that afternoon, Sherlock couldn't shake the feeling that something was off. He typed out another search: "Dustin Dieber missing lie." Another list of results appeared. The first article was from a national investigative foundation (www.findpeople.org) with the title "Dustin Dieber Is NOT Missing! Learn More about the Lie That Has Consumed SocialGram." *Yes.* "Bingo," Sherlock whispered, clicking on the page. He began to read:

> (Los Angeles, California)—A few days ago, world-famous musician and actor Dustin Dieber was reported missing by @DustinDieberFans, a popular Dustin Dieber fan page on social media platform SocialGram. Within hours, the post went viral, and millions of fans were plunged into what they labeled "#DustinDoom." In fact, the first post was meant to be a practical joke. The account owner posted a correction, but it was too late: false messages spread across the internet, with some fans organizing search parties, and others holding candlelit vigils. Unfortunately, the lie coincided with Dustin's decision to remain at his home in Los Angeles, where he is currently "spending time with family" after the passing of a relative.

Sherlock felt himself grinning. *Dustin isn't missing . . . It was all a lie!* He glanced down at the entry in his notebook. That tip had come in handy. And because of it, he had just solved his first mystery! He immediately printed the article and ran downstairs. "Mom?"

He found his mom in the living room, watching her all-time favorite movie—*Dustin Dieber: The Documentary*—and crying. Next to her, his dad was consoling her. "I know, sweetie. But they really don't know anything yet. We just need to wait and see." When he saw Sherlock, he frowned, as if to say, *Thanks for doing this*.

Wait until he sees this, Sherlock thought. He took a deep breath. "Guys! I solved the Dustin Dieber case!" he announced.

His parents looked up, startled. Ken poked his head out from the kitchen, snickering. "Here we go again . . ." He laughed. "I can't wait for this. What is it this time? The neighbors hate Dustin, so they kidnapped him?"

Sherlock's dad sighed deeply. "Sherlock, I'm not sure now is the time for—"

"He's not missing!" Sherlock half yelled. He'd planned a whole lead-up, but like any good detective, he knew how to read a room—and when his window of opportunity was closing.

"What?" his mom asked, dumbfounded.

Sherlock handed her the article and began to talk through his findings. "And that's why no one's spotted him, Mom!" he concluded. "Because he's at home with his family, not because he's missing."

His family stared intently at him. *This is usually the time that something goes wrong*, Sherlock thought. He waited to hear Ken snicker, or to see his dad shake his head. Instead, a second later, he found himself wrapped in a bear hug from his mom. *Oh jeez.*

"My incredible little detective!" she said through tears. "Did you see that, Roh?" she asked Sherlock's dad. "He figured it out!"

His dad nodded, patting him on the back. "Good job fact-checking your mother, son," he whispered, winking.

Sherlock laughed. Even Ken gave him a high five. "Nice. Now we don't have to listen to Mom drone on about this for the next week." Behind him, Sherlock's mom swatted him.

"Piece of advice, Mom?" Sherlock said to her. "Don't trust everything you read online. And before you share something on SocialGram, you should check to see if it's true . . . especially if it's from diebergossip.com." Next to him, his dad and Ken chortled.

His mom blushed . . . and then nodded. "Okay, okay . . . You're right, Sherlock. Thank you."

And he was! *If that isn't a mystery solved, I don't know what is,* Sherlock thought triumphantly. Case closed.

CHAPTER 3 INTERNET CHALLENGE

Congratulations on completing chapter 3! You're well on your way to becoming a digital detective. 🕵️

Amid the soybean sprouts soup, chicken parmesan (with a side of danger), and doctor's appointments, Sherlock Solver's story highlighted why keeping an eye out for misinformation—or false information—especially online, is so, so important. Maybe, like Isaiah, you have an allergy—and know that the effects of a bite of contaminated food really suck. In any case, as Sherlock learned, a high follower count or handsome smile does not a trustworthy source make. *Dr. Rong's Food Encyclopedia* was very deceiving—and even fooled Sherlock's mom! The lesson is: **anyone can be a victim of false information online—don't let it be you**. Sherlock was ultimately able to crack the Dustin Dieber case by using the digital detective tips we discussed: finding a recent, reliable, and unbiased source. You certainly couldn't say that about the @DustinDieberFans SocialGram page!

Now that you've read Sherlock's story, it's time for you to get on the case! Practice detecting whether a source on the internet is reliable or not. First, find an article, image, or video that a friend or family member shared recently. Then, using the digital detective tips, determine whether the source is reputable and the content is trustworthy. Try to back up your reasoning with the tips as a guide. Share your findings with your friend or family member!

POST?

CHAPTER 4
ARE YOU *SURE* YOU WANT TO POST THAT?

N ow and then, you might wonder: Who invented the internet? The answer to that question is very long (just know it involved some pretty cool folks!), but it should remind you: it was a bunch of people—people like you and me—who built the internet. When the internet was first invented, though, many of those folks had no idea how people would use it ten, twenty, or five hundred years later. They weren't fortune-tellers! As time passed, things changed—more and more folks got online, social media was born, and the internet became a super important part of our lives. Unfortunately, the internet's design didn't change with it, making it a less-than-perfect fit for our new world. The result? Nowadays, sometimes it can feel like what we say or do online . . . just doesn't matter. After all, there's *so* much else out there—what are the odds that your post is going to go viral? And your words aren't permanent: if you change your mind, you can just delete the message, right? Unfortunately, not quite. In a world where anyone can screenshot your message and information is shared at lightning speed, it's more important than ever that you rethink before hitting SEND. So the next time you're about to post something, stop, pause, and rethink: Are you sure you want to post that? With just a few extra seconds to reflect, you can outsmart the internet.

"Folks, it's now eight p.m. here in New York City. The votes are in! We'll have the results in a few moments. Please stay with us." The newscaster flashed a smile, and a second later, the show cut to an ad break. As a jingle about breakfast cereal began to play, Aiyden John Commander—"AJ" to his friends and family—swallowed nervously. He could feel pools of sweat collecting on his palms. *The results are in. This is it.* He was about to find out if over two years of hard work had finally paid off. *What if it hasn't? What will I do?*

He felt a hand on his shoulder; startled, he looked up. *Oh.* It was his older sister, Ayesha. She laughed at his reaction. "Calm down, little man! It's just me—your favorite sister." AJ laughed in response—Ayesha was his only sister—but was soon distracted by the sound of the TV. The biggest moment of his life was just a few minutes away. Sensing his nerves, Ayesha patted him gently. "You have nothing to worry about, AJ," she said, and smiled. "You're going to win—I know it." AJ heard murmurs of assent, followed by loud *whoops* and prayers; energized, he felt a sense of excitement course through his veins. *I hope they're right.*

As if on cue, the TV station's theme music began to play. *This is it.* Around him, AJ's friends and family linked arms. He took his mother's hand and then Ayesha's; turning to the TV, he exhaled deeply. *No matter what*, he thought, *it was worth it. Every moment of this was worth it.*

On the TV, the newscaster smiled broadly. "Good evening, everyone, and thank you for tuning in to NewsLive. My name is Kristof Reportor. Just a few moments ago, polls across the nation closed—and the results are now in. Our experts are projecting that . . . Aiyden John Commander, a politician from New Orleans, Louisiana, will be the next president of the United States! Let's turn now to some analysis from our commentators . . ."

The newscaster's words were drowned out by the cheers that erupted in the room. AJ was stunned. *I won. I really won!* His friends and family rapidly encircled him, chanting his name. "AJ! AJ! AJ!" His best friend, Karina—also his pick for vice president—came running up to him. The two high-fived, and Karina pulled him in for a hug. "Yes, dude! We did it," she said, beaming. In that moment, AJ felt invincible. He'd achieved his lifelong dream—and now he could make change for millions. Around him, the chanting grew louder. "AJ! AJ!"

"AJ! Aiyden John Commander! Get up, now!" *Wait. That*

71

doesn't sound quite right . . . What is that? AJ's eyes slowly opened. Disoriented, he looked around; the TV was still in front of him, but the room was empty . . . until his mama walked in, her hands on her hips. "Don't make me tell you twice, AJ! You and Ayesha are leaving in five minutes. Get off that couch, *now!*"

Oh . . . Disappointed, AJ flopped back onto the couch. *It was just a dream.* He closed his eyes again, hoping to capture just a few more moments. He could still faintly hear his name, along with the cheers of a waiting crowd . . . *One day, AJ,* he thought. *One day, that'll be you. But right now . . .* he needed to get up, before his mama lit into him again. Mustering all of his energy, he finally slinked off the couch, hastily grabbed a pair of sneakers, and walked out onto his driveway, where his sister was waiting for him.

AJ was only in the seventh grade at Leadership Academy, but he had plenty of ambition. He already knew what he wanted to be when he grew up: the president of the United States! He remembered when he'd first decided on that: a few years earlier, his teacher, Mr. Archive, had taught a unit on the presidents of the United States. AJ was in awe of their accomplishments (even if he thought some of their choices could've been improved). He immediately knew that *he* wanted to be in the big history textbook one day, with students learning about all of the important decisions he'd made. And looking at the pictures of the presidents on the classroom tapestry, he thought it'd be nice if there were a few more who looked like him.

Even though the US presidency was years away—he had to wait to run until he was thirty-five!—now AJ had a chance to do something similar: serve as the president of the student council! The election was set for the week after winter break ended—and since Christmas, AJ had been in planning mode. With his daddy's help, he'd put together an election platform and planning list; with Ayesha, he'd watched every political-thriller movie the family owned. And, of course, AJ had studied his No. 1 political hero: the local mayor, Mr. Hugh Mouth. Mr. Mouth had been the mayor of the town for years. His supporters absolutely loved him, and AJ could see why: he was charismatic, he was smart, he created policies that made the town better, and he had a great smile, something AJ's mama loved to point out (which made AJ's daddy roll his eyes). Mr. Mouth was in the midst of an election too! He was running to be reelected as town mayor. Speaking of which . . . *He's hosting his last Q and A event later today*, AJ remembered. *I definitely need to go to that.* AJ planned to take lots of notes . . . and hopefully, he'd be able to channel Mr. Mouth for *his* campaign.

In spite of all his prep, AJ was still nervous . . . There was so much left to do, and . . . *if I'm being honest, I have no idea if I'm doing any of it right.* In all of the movies he'd watched, the politicians always had some special secret—a fancy way of talking or a killer attention to detail—that was the key to their success. Mr. Mouth, it seemed, had several! AJ had no idea what his special secret was—or if he even had one. Now,

73

walking along the path into town with his sister, AJ felt his doubts begin to consume him. *What if I never find it? And . . . what if I lose?*

Ayesha glanced at him. "Are you okay, little man? You seem worked up about something."

AJ shook his head. "I don't know what you're talking about."

Ayesha raised her eyebrows, skeptical.

"Just leave me alone, Ayesha!" AJ said, frustrated.

Ayesha threw her hands up in defeat. "Gosh, AJ. There's no need to be so hostile. Okay, okay . . . if you say so."

A second later, AJ sighed. "Okay, fine . . . I'm sorry. I'm nervous about the election. It's just . . . I have no idea what I'm doing. I don't have any student council experience! Maybe I stink," he said. Then, the thought that'd been worrying him for the past week: "Maybe I'm not right for this."

Ayesha suddenly stopped walking. Confused, AJ did too. *What is she doing?* Peering down at him over her glasses, Ayesha looked him square in the eyes. "You don't stink, AJ, and you can do this—I promise. Let me help you," she said.

AJ wrinkled his nose. *My sister, helping me? Sounds kinda lame.*

"Most politicians have several people helping them," Ayesha continued. "I'll be like . . . your campaign manager." AJ brightened— *That actually sounds kind of cool.* "I'll keep you organized and on track. And as a thank-you, you can buy me dessert at Nomnom's!" Ayesha loved Nomnom's ice cream—they all did; it was the best in town. *Fair enough, AJ*

 74

thought. He'd never had his sister help him before . . . or wanted her to, but he was desperate. He stuck out his hand, and they shook.

"It's a deal," AJ said. "Thank you."

"Don't thank me yet," Ayesha said. "We have, well, a *lot* of work to do . . . So, what's first on your planning list?" AJ's forehead crinkled. *How does she know about that?* "I saw it on the kitchen counter," Ayesha said, smiling. *Is she laughing at me?* AJ scowled. "And—for the record—I think it's a great idea," she said quickly. "So . . . what's first on the list?"

AJ sighed. *Here we go.* "I need to buy a suit for my campaign rally . . . Is there a store around here somewhere?"

Ayesha nodded authoritatively. "Yes, sir . . . Let's get you suited up!"

An hour later, they'd left Suits and Suave, the local tailor shop, with not one suit, but three suits in tow! AJ had to admit—Ayesha had outdone herself. The first few suits had been a disaster; either the coat was too big, the pants too short, or the colors off. It was only thanks to Ayesha, who'd spied a few suits on the "unconventional" rack, that AJ now had the Patriot Collection: one blue suit, one white suit, and one red suit, each with star designs in the stitches. Even better, he'd gotten the only set left in the store! *I have my "special ingredient" covered.* As he and Ayesha walked out onto Main Street, AJ finally felt confident about his run . . . that is, until he rounded the corner, where he stopped dead in his tracks.

Next to him, Ayesha cocked her head. "Is that . . . Igor Bossy?" she asked, her voice wary. It was! Igor was in AJ's homeroom at the academy. AJ didn't like him much; he was constantly telling people what to do, even if they hadn't asked. And his "tips" weren't helpful—or nice. Before winter break, Igor had told AJ to "get a haircut, Commander! Your hair's a complete disaster," while the class howled. Now it seemed AJ's worst nightmare had come true: Igor was leaving Suits Galore, the other suit shop in town—and he was holding a Patriot Collection set of suits! When he noticed AJ, he smirked. "See you on the campaign stage, Commander!" he yelled out. A second later, he was gone.

I'm going up against Igor Bossy, AJ realized. "Crud," he said out loud, sighing. Igor was a member of the "in" crowd at school; how could AJ ever hope to beat that? Forget a collection of friends; he couldn't even rely on his suits . . . Looking down at them, AJ felt himself deflate. *So much for a secret weapon*, AJ thought dejectedly.

"Don't worry about him," Ayesha instructed.

AJ rolled his eyes. "Easy for you to say! Igor Bossy . . . well, he's the king of the school."

Ayesha shook her head. "*Was* the king. He won't be anymore . . . after you win."

AJ sighed. "I'm not going to win! He even has the same suits."

"So what?" Ayesha countered. "Let's find you another advantage."

Next on the list was his slogan. On the walk home, AJ

refined it with Ayesha. "I don't get it," AJ complained, exasperated. "What's wrong with 'If you want free candy, vote for AJ!'? It's catchy and . . . everyone loves candy. It's foolproof."

Ayesha shook her head. "You say 'foolproof,' I say 'boring.' We need something *creative*." After fifteen minutes of quibbling, they finally settled on "Vote for AJ: your wish is his . . . Command!" AJ had to admit it was pretty good. And later this afternoon, he had the Q and A with Mayor Mouth! *Maybe my run isn't completely hopeless.*

When he got home, AJ headed straight to his bedroom. *Time for the Q and A with Mayor Mouth!* On his desk was the flyer for the event: "Come one, come all! Your mayor, Mr. Hugh Mouth, will be hosting a Q and A before the mayoral election tomorrow. Don't forget to join on www.socialbook.com! The Q and A starts at four p.m. Don't be late!" *A social media Q and A is a pretty smart idea, especially for an old guy,* AJ thought. *Of course, Mr. Mouth is the smartest!*

Above AJ, the clock read 3:57. AJ grabbed his planning notebook and pen, and quickly powered on his laptop, logging in to his SocialBook account, @AJThePresident. There it was, under the EVENTS tab: **MR. HUGH MOUTH'S PRE-ELECTION Q and A!** *Perfect.*

Instantly, a picture of Mr. Mouth appeared on the screen. In it, he was wearing a crisp blue suit, complete with a striped blue-and-white tie, and flashing his signature smile. *His teeth*

really are perfect, AJ thought. *Maybe I should actually brush my teeth for two minutes every morning like Mama always tells me to . . .* "Noted," AJ whispered to himself, making an entry in his notebook.

Next to the image of Mr. Mouth was a large chat box where folks could submit questions for the Q and A; there were already several questions in the box. "How will your proposed tax increases affect middle-income workers?" read one question. "Why don't you support a new fountain in the city park?" said another. AJ sighed. *So boring.* Though . . . he could ask a question of his own, he realized. He clicked on the box and carefully typed: "What's the most important lesson you've learned in your career as a politician?"

Suddenly, there was a flash, and the image came to life. It was Mr. Mouth, in the same outfit—*and he looks just as good*, AJ thought, amazed. "Good afternoon, everyone!" Mr. Mouth said loudly. He looked lost, staring at random parts of his computer screen. *Why is he doing that?* "My name is Hugh Mouth, and I'm here today—before yet another election—to answer your questions. But I'd like to begin by telling you all why I'm running . . ." Some of it was kind of cheesy—he made a couple of dad jokes—but just like AJ's mama always said, he sure was charming!

After he finished talking, Mr. Mouth paused. "With that, I'll begin taking questions. Remember, you can see me, but I can't see all of you, so if you have follow-ups or want to share something else, just drop a note in the chat, and I'll respond." *Oh. That's why he looked so confused earlier—he can't*

see us. That's a weird setup, AJ thought, *but okay . . . I guess.*

"The first question is from Joe Manchego, of the Cheeseline subdivision. The question is 'Why should we vote for you?' You know, that's a great question, Joe . . ." *A great question? Please. It was terrible . . . and yet, Mr. Mouth made the answer sound so good.* AJ made another entry in his notebook: "Be prepared for good *and* bad questions."

Wait . . . what was that?! Suddenly, the chat box was flooded with messages.

@JinyanUnhappie: **Don't vote for Hugh Mouth! Our town deserves better!**

@KarenVexed: **Down with No Action Hugh!**

It was a planned invasion from Mr. Mouth's opposition! Several of the comments were from people AJ didn't know, but one was from none other than Igor Bossy! *Of course . . . he joined too.* Igor's message was, as always, in desperate need of creativity: @IgorTHEBOSSBossy: **Mr. Mouth is OUT!**

AJ rolled his eyes. But it was working—no one was paying attention to Mr. Mouth, AJ realized; the messages had stolen the show.

Mr. Mouth must've realized it, too, because he abruptly stopped talking. "For this next question on our city's taxes, I'm going to hand it off to my treasurer and financial director, Ms. Lorna Cash," he said shortly. "That'll give me some time to respond to these . . . new messages." *He's super angry*, AJ realized. Mr. Mouth's face was flushed, his eyes were narrowed, and his expression was steely.

Another message rolled in. @RicoS: **Mr. Hugh Mouth is**

not what this town needs! We need fresh thinking, creativity, and change. Vote for Diane Shift! A second later,
the computer beeped. An alert appeared: HOST MESSAGE. Mr.
Mouth had sent something in the chat! *He's probably saved
the day!* AJ eagerly peered at the message . . . and gasped.

It read, @MAYORMOUTH: **Why would anyone listen to
YOU, Rico? Have you done anything for this town and its
people? NOPE. Go find something better to do . . . Oh, wait,
that's right. You're a big-time loser! Sorry, buddy . . . but
I'm not sorry. What a MORON.**

AJ was shocked. *Why would Mr. Mouth say something like
that?!* AJ obviously didn't know him, but he'd always seemed
like a calm, collected guy. He could hardly imagine Mr.
Mouth—who, to AJ, had always been the perfect politician—
actually saying something like that. *Isn't taking feedback—even
if it isn't the nicest—part of his job?* It seemed that Mr. Mouth
had been going for a laugh . . . *But it really wasn't that funny*, AJ
thought. *More like . . . super harsh and not really justified.* And it
made Mr. Mouth look so unprofessional. *Unless . . . that's the
lesson here?* AJ wondered, his forehead crinkling. *Is that Mr.
Mouth's special ingredient? Is that what I have to do too?*

Suddenly, AJ heard his computer beep again. 1 NEW NO-
TIFICATION ON SOCIALBOOK: LOCAL HASHTAG TRENDING. AJ
clicked on the notification. Instantly, he was staring at a col-
lage of posts sharing the hashtag "#MouthOff" . . . and all of
them included a screenshot of Mr. Mouth's chat message!
**So disappointing to see Mayor Mouth respond to a *child's*
comment this way**, read one post. **Is this who you want at**

the helm of our city? It's time for change. Vote for Diane Shift. #MouthOff. AJ's heart dropped. *This cannot be good for Mr. Mouth . . .* The posts soon went viral—every time AJ refreshed his page, it seemed that at least another thousand people in town had seen them. *Okay, so, clearly* not *the thing to do*, AJ thought. *Noted . . . no notebook necessary.*

Wait . . . why did that post refer to a "child"? AJ scrolled through a few of the other posts, until . . . *No way.* With bated breath, he clicked on a #MouthOff post written by a user named Rico S. *The same name as the user who sent the initial message to Mr. Mouth!* It was then that AJ realized . . . "Rico S" was Rico Shift, Diane Shift's son! Rico went to Activist Academy, the other middle school in town. He was AJ's age—just thirteen years old! AJ couldn't believe it. Mr. Mouth hadn't just messed up . . . He'd *really* messed up. *He straight-up attacked a kid—who happens to be the son of his opponent!* It was a complete disaster.

AJ heard the door to his room open. It was Ayesha, phone in hand. "Have you seen this hashtag that's going around?" she asked, confused. "What's '#MouthOff'? What did he do?"

After AJ had finished explaining, Ayesha shook her head. "Wow . . . See, AJ? *That's* why it doesn't pay to be like Igor Bossy. And why you better watch your mouth," she said, her face serious.

AJ laughed, indignant. "Do you think I'd ever be that stupid?" he asked.

Ayesha sighed. "That's the thing, AJ—I don't think he was thinking," she said. "You'd better not do that."

81

As she turned and left, AJ swiveled back to his computer. *Ayesha's right.* He knew Mr. Mouth was so much better than that message. *And yet . . . one bad decision probably just cost Mr. Mouth the election.* Just thinking about it made AJ sick to his stomach.

AJ quickly toggled back to the SocialBook Q and A. *Mr. Mouth has got to have figured this out . . . after all, he's . . . the best,* AJ thought. *Right?* In fact, that didn't seem to be the case. On the screen, a pink-faced Mr. Mouth was at a loss for words. (AJ couldn't remember ever having seen him like this! Nor did he think anyone else had.) Finally, Mr. Mouth cleared his throat. "Ahem . . . Folks . . . erm . . . I see now that there's a new hashtag circulating on SocialBook . . . and . . . um . . . well, I'd like to address these claims here and now, while I have the chance. I deeply apologize for my message earlier—I was frustrated, and angry, because this was supposed to be a space for me and my supporters after a difficult election season. I assure you . . . that those words do not represent who I am! I just— Well . . . I don't even know! I lost control, and I wasn't thinking. To Rico, Diane, and their family, I'm so very sorry."

In response, messages began to pop up in the chat box.

@VISHALFURIUS: **How are we supposed to trust you?**

@MARKFOOMING: **Apology NOT accepted. Why would you ever say something like that?**

@SHIRAHURT: **I've campaigned for you for 4 months! You should've known better!**

@TAMARAWRATH: **Do you not think you're accountable for what you say?**

On the screen, Mr. Mouth seemed to shrink. "Uh . . . and with that, I'll need to cut this afternoon short. Thank you all so much for joining me, and I'll see you at the polls tomorrow! Don't forget: there's no doubt—your candidate is Mouth." *Click*. In a flash, the video was gone, and AJ was staring at a message: YOUR EVENT IS OVER.

And so is Mr. Mouth's campaign, AJ thought.

By the time AJ woke up the next morning, Mr. Mouth had already released a statement apologizing again for the message—and announcing he was dropping out of the race. Diane Shift would win the election by default; Ayesha told them all about it at breakfast. "Huh," AJ's mama clucked. "Well, I never would've expected it from him, but here we are. Anyway . . ." She turned to AJ. "Speaking of elections, Aiyden . . . how's the preparation coming?"

"He's running against Igor Bossy," Ayesha informed them as she slathered butter on her toast. "Oh, and I'm his campaign manager, so all questions can be directed to me. I'm basically the reason he has a shot at all," she announced as their mama swatted her. AJ rolled his eyes.

"It's going good, Mama," AJ said. "I actually think I figured out what I'm doing for my social media campaign!" The social media campaign was perhaps the most important part of the election; last year, it had pretty much decided the winners (understandably, because all of his classmates spent a

ton of time on SocialBook). AJ knew he had to get it right . . .
And I'm pretty sure I have, he thought happily.

"Oh?" AJ's daddy asked. "And what's that, son?"

"I'm going to do a series of open-feedback events on
SocialBook. Each one will hit on a key part of my platform—
adding candy to the school lunches, homework limits, and
more. People at school can join and tell me what *they* want
to see. And . . . that'll be my secret weapon," AJ said, the realization coming to him as he spoke. "Everyone expects me
to do all the talking, but this way, I'll give them a chance
to share how they're feeling—and it'll make them feel like
they can trust me, because I'm all about them." He smiled.
"Meanwhile, Igor Bossy will be so busy admiring himself, he
won't know what hit him!" Everyone at the table laughed.

"Gotta hand it to you, little man," Ayesha said. "That's
pretty dang smart. Better than what I could've come up
with." (She sounded a little disappointed.)

"Attaboy!" his daddy said. "You got it going, man!"

AJ felt himself fill with pride. *I do got this*, he thought.
Glancing at the poster from Mr. Mouth's event the day before, he realized, *And I definitely got it more than him.* Suffice
it to say, Mr. Mouth was no longer AJ's political role model.
Mr. Mouth should've thought more carefully about his.

He looked over at Ayesha. She arched her eyebrows.
"So . . . Nomnom's?"

AJ laughed. "Yeah, yeah, Nomnom's . . ." *And maybe another scoop after I win.*

CHAPTER 4 INTERNET CHALLENGE

You just completed chapter 4—nice job! You're well on your way to becoming a pro at rethinking your words online.

AJ might be years away from his run for the presidency, but as you read in chapter 4, he's already learned the most important lesson there is: **being intentional about what you say—online and offline—really matters**. Indeed, amid his rivalry with Igor Bossy, his killer campaign slogan, and dreams of victory, underlying AJ's story was the importance of taking the time to rethink before hitting SEND. Even his hero, Mr. Mouth—an adult who "should've known better"—got carried away online, in an environment that made it easy to do the wrong thing. Unable to see the folks he was speaking to, his anger boiled over. Later, Mr. Mouth tried to take the comments back, but screenshots were already circulating all over the internet with the hashtag "#MouthOff"—the damage was done. Had he taken a moment to pause and rethink, he could've saved his reputation—and the election!

Now that you've finished this chapter and read AJ's story, it's your turn to rethink what you say online. It's not easy to outsmart the internet, so celebrate every win! The next time you successfully rethink a message, share one of the custom messages below (or something similar) on your social media, and encourage your friends to do the same, using the hashtags "#ThinkBeforeYouType" and "#InternetSuperhero." See my personalized post for an example!

Custom messages:

No matter what, we can always be kind.

#ThinkBeforeYouType—good vibes only, please! 💕

For everyone who needs to hear it today: you are better than all of the negativity in the world and on social media. Love yourself! 🖤 And for everyone else, #ThinkBeforeYouType—your words matter.

Kindness is never overrated. Your words can change a life. Be an #InternetSuperhero, and #ThinkBeforeYouType!

Trisha's post:

@TrishPrabhu: These past few months have been tough, and it's been hard to stay positive, but I've tried to keep the #GoodVibes going 🖤. So for anyone who needs to hear it today: you are better than all of the negativity out there, in the world and on social media. #ThinkBeforeYouType, and spread a little love!

CHAPTER 5
IF YOU SEE SOMETHING, SAY SOMETHING

The internet is far from perfect. Even if you follow all of the rules, there's a good chance other folks—kids, or even adults, like your parents—won't. *Great*, you're probably thinking. *What do I do about that?* Here's the answer: Be an upstander, someone who uses your voice to advocate for a kinder, more respectful internet. In other words, if you see something that isn't right, take a stand. Maybe it's something obvious, like a rude comment on a picture. Maybe it's something more subtle, like a joke in a group chat that isn't super funny anymore. No matter what it is, use your voice to say that it isn't okay and set an example for your friends, family, and community. *But, Trisha, wait . . . that sounds so uncool. Plus, what if people laugh at me?* Trust me, I get it!

Being an upstander can sometimes be out of your comfort zone. But being a leader—and leading with compassion and empathy—is actually one of the coolest things you can do. Just ask Greta Thunberg and Malala Yousafzai: Greta is a nineteen-year-old Swedish activist fighting to raise awareness about climate change, and Malala is an ambassador for educating girls in Pakistan and around the globe! They both saw problems in the world and decided to act. By being an upstander, you can too.

The last bell of the day rang. "Okay, class!" Mrs. Math said. "Don't forget—your math test is on Monday!"

Finally, Kristin Artiste thought. *The weekend!* That meant time to paint in her art studio, watch her favorite romantic movies with Daisy, her golden retriever, and *not* be here, at Dramatique Middle School. And as for that math test, she wasn't worried. She had the highest grade in the class.

Tayshia Bestie, Kristin's best friend, cleared her desk and made her way over to Kristin. "It's the weekend," she trilled. "I thought Mrs. Math would never stop talking. Want to come over and do each other's nails?"

Kristin turned to respond, but the words never left her mouth. Suddenly, she couldn't speak. Her feet were glued to the ground, and her heart was pounding. She felt her face getting red. "Erhm . . ." she said.

"Kristin? What are you looking at?" Tayshia asked, trying

to follow her line of gaze around the classroom. But Kristin wasn't staring at something; she was staring at someone . . .

Juan Lipsmacker.

Juan was in the sixth grade—just like Kristin and Tayshia. He was, undoubtedly, the cutest, coolest guy in the grade. From his leather jacket (imported from Spain!) to his warm brown eyes, he was the ultimate catch. He was also so nice, and he told the best jokes. Everyone liked Juan. And so many people wanted Juan to like them—especially Kristin. She closed her eyes and replayed the dream she'd had about him for months, inspired by her all-time favorite romantic movie, *The Greatest Love Story*. There he was—Juan, in a tuxedo, holding a box of caramel chocolates (Kristin's favorite). "Strong, smart Kristin," he said. "You have captured all of me. Will you be mine, Kristin?"

"Yes . . ." Kristin mumbled dreamily.

"Kristin?"

Kristin's eyes flew open. In front of her, Juan was staring at her, looking worried. "Are you okay?"

Kristin turned a bright shade of red—almost purple. "Yes!" she spluttered. "I was just"—*Think, Kristin, think!*—"meditating," she announced to the departing class, a few of whom glanced back at her. "It's really good for you, in case you were wondering!"

Juan smiled. "Gotcha—that's cool," he said, sounding impressed, before walking away. Kristin sighed. *Crisis averted . . . almost!* In the back of the class, Akari Giggles, Mila Chuckles, and Ida Teaser, who had all been watching, burst out laughing. *Argh*, Kristin thought. Next to them, Lisa Rabblerouser cocked her head curiously, staring at Kristin as if she were trying to figure something out. Kristin flushed.

"And . . . I'm late! I gotta go." Kristin fled. The weekend couldn't have come soon enough!

"Kristin, wait!" Tayshia yelled.

Outside, Kristin stopped to brush away a tear. *How humiliating*, she thought. *Juan must think I'm an absolute dweeb. And he wouldn't be wrong.* As if on cue, Tayshia, who had just caught up to her, said, between pants, "Juan . . . doesn't . . . think . . . you're . . . a . . . dweeb!"

"Yes, he does!" Kristin moaned. "And even worse, Lisa is onto me. She knows I like Juan!"

Tayshia waved her hand. "It'll be old news by Monday. Akari, Mila, Ida, and Lisa will have caught wind of some other scandal." *I hope so*, Kristin thought.

"But, Kristin . . ." Tayshia said. "A word of advice?" Kristin looked up at her. "Don't daydream in class." Kristin rolled her eyes, and after a moment, they both snorted and started laughing.

But, Kristin spent that weekend worrying— *What if Lisa has figured it out?* She'd never be able to live it down. Tayshia was right; she needed to be careful. But it was so hard! Every time she saw Juan, she was immediately transported to one of the romantic movies she loved so much, complete with the background music and costumes. *Although*, Kristin thought, *maybe that's the problem*—she spent too much time watching those movies!

What I need to do is find a way to control my crush before I do another embarrassing thing in front of Juan! So Kristin tried to distract herself by taking Daisy for a walk, and even studying for her math test (fractions were so easy . . . and boring). She texted Tayshia, and the two of them went to see a movie and play arcade games. And, of course, she spent a ton of time on SocialGram, scrolling through picture after picture. Even that wasn't enough—by Sunday evening, she'd run out of things to do (argh!)—and she needed a plan before the start of the new week.

"What do you think, Daisy? What should I do?" she asked her dog. Daisy barked and tugged at Kristin's arm. "Daisy!" Kristin laughed. "What are you doing, you old girl?" Daisy tugged again, harder this time, and jumped down from the couch. Kristin followed her—up from the basement, across the house, and out into the backyard—to her art studio. *Of course*, Kristin realized. How had she not thought of it? She'd paint. Next to her, Daisy barked happily. "That's my good girl," Kristin said, giving her a big hug.

Inside her art studio, Kristin instantly felt calmer. The studio was familiar and smelled like opportunity, with the scent of pastels, watercolors, drying canvases, and old brushes blending together. It was Kristin's happy place. She loved art—for as long as she could remember, she'd been painting (including on the walls of her house, which her

91

parents hadn't been happy about). Using the great artists of the past—among them, Pablo Picasso and Frida Kahlo—as inspiration, she'd developed her own style. Her favorite things to paint? Places, people, and moments filled with emotion. She remembered the painting she'd done after her team had won the local soccer championship in the fifth grade—she had been so excited, proud, and triumphant. Whenever her feelings consumed her, she turned to her art. And through her art, she found a place to express herself.

Kristin turned on some music, pulled out a blank canvas, and placed it on the stand before her. Without thinking, she began to draw, sketching an outline and letting her feelings guide her. The outline quickly took the form of Juan—a portrait. *Perfect*, Kristin thought. Around him, Kristin drew everything she felt when she saw Juan: fireworks, stars, and hearts. After she finished the outline, she began to paint, mixing colors, sharpening lines, and covering up any smudges.

Three hours and one paint-splattered T-shirt later, the painting was finished. Juan smiled down at her, with cartoonlike hearts in his warm brown eyes. *I love it*, Kristin thought happily. *Nice work, Kristin.*

She grabbed a Sharpie and bent down to sign the painting. Suddenly, she hesitated. *What if, somehow, Juan finds this?* "Nah," she said out loud. "How could he? It's never leaving this studio." She signed it with a flourish: "Kristin Annabel Artiste."

She took a picture of the painting and texted it to Tayshia.

> My love has no bounds 🖤

A few seconds later, Tayshia responded:

> You're crazy . . . in love! That's straight-up amazing. My best friend is SO talented!

Kristin beamed with pride.

The next day, Kristin found herself in a good mood. When her science teacher, Mr. Bio, said they'd have double homework that evening, she barely blinked. And when she accidentally spilled chocolate milk on her favorite T-shirt at lunch, she didn't even notice. "What's wrong with you?" Tayshia asked curiously. "You're acting . . . different."

"Nothing!" Kristin said quickly. "You're bananas," she added dismissively, for good measure.

It wasn't nothing . . . it was the painting. That morning before school, Kristin had visited it again in her studio. In the early morning light, it was clear: it was one of her best pieces. The colors, the design, the lighting—it was all absolutely perfect. Kristin had been so proud. *And even better*, Kristin thought now, *because of it, I've stopped staring at Juan all the time*—now that she had a painting, she didn't have to look at him! *Mission accomplished.*

Of course, it seemed wrong to *never* look at someone who

was so perfect . . . and so, during free period, like everyone else, Kristin pulled out her phone and pretended to check SocialGram, but instead, sneaked a glance at Juan across the classroom. *Hold on.* Kristin squinted at Juan. *Is it just me, or is his brown hair much lighter than I'd thought? Darn—I messed up my painting.* She pulled up the picture of it on her phone, trying to assess how far off she'd been. *It's not too bad—just a few shades off. Maybe I can fix it after school. Soccer practice, and then homework, but I should have an hour before dinn—*

"Whatcha doing, Kristin?" a voice interrupted her. Startled, Kristin dropped her phone onto her desk. Lisa Rabblerouser stood in front of her. Kristin flushed.

"What were you looking at just now?" Lisa asked, smiling broadly.

"N-nothing," Kristin stammered. "I was just—checking SocialGram."

"Really?" Lisa asked, feigning an interested tone and smiling even wider now.

"Yeah," Kristin said nervously. "Anyway—I have to use the bathroom." She half sprinted to her teacher's desk ("I *need* to use the restroom!") and then out the door. In the bathroom, she stared at her reflection, panic roiling in her stomach. *Hold on.* Kristin took a few deep breaths. *What could Lisa have seen, honestly? She was probably just messing with you.* As she walked back to class, Kristin calmed down. She refused to let Lisa get to her, even if Lisa was one of the most popular girls at school. *And nothing bad happened, really.*

The bell rang. It was time for Kristin's next class—

math—and the big math test. "All right, class," Mrs. Math said. "Let's see how well you've mastered this material. As a reminder, please turn off your cell phones now and put them away! If I see a phone out during the test, you will lose points—no exceptions."

Kristin grabbed her phone to turn it off and saw a text message from Tayshia. Curious, she quickly tapped on it.

> Tayshia: DID YOU SEE THIS?!

Suddenly, another message appeared.

> Tayshia: WHY DID YOU SEND LISA YOUR PAINTING?

Kristin's eyes widened. She opened Tayshia's texts, and gasped. There it was: a screenshot of Lisa's latest post on SocialGram . . . Kristin's painting of Juan! Lisa had captioned it, **Someone has a big crush on @JuanLipsmack30!** Clearly visible at the bottom of the painting was Kristin's signature. At first, Kristin was confused: How could this be? Then, she realized— *The bathroom!* When she'd gone to the bathroom, Lisa had picked up her phone—still unlocked and open on the picture of Juan—and sent the picture to herself! She checked her sent messages, and sure enough, there it was. From Kristin Artiste to Lisa Rabblerouser, with the caption: 😏.

Kristin felt faint. This couldn't be happening. If they hadn't already, the whole school would see her painting!

Including Juan—he was tagged in the picture! Her. Life. Was. Over.

She looked helplessly over at Tayshia. Tayshia frowned at her and signaled with her eyes, as if to say, *Put your phone in your backpack.*

Huh? Kristin thought.

"Kristin Artiste." Mrs. Math's voice pierced the room.

Uh-oh. Kristin froze. *That's what Tayshia was trying to say.*

She looked up at Mrs. Math and felt herself wilt under her—appropriately—fiery gaze. "Mrs. Math, I'm so sorry. I wasn't listening, and—"

"That's right, Miss Artiste," Mrs. Math said. "You weren't listening. I clearly told the class to put their phones away! I'm very disappointed in you, Kristin," she said, her eyes narrowing. "This is so unlike you. In any case, five points will be deducted from your exam." As she walked away, she said more loudly, "And let this serve as a warning to everyone. Put those abominable phones away!"

Kristin felt like throwing up. *Lose points?* She'd never gotten anything lower than an A on a math test before! This was all because of . . . She turned around furiously and searched with her eyes for Lisa . . . and there she was, in the back. Kristin stared at her angrily. Lisa looked up from her exam and laughed silently at Kristin's expression. Next to her, Akari, Mila, and Ida looked up too. Even worse, so did a few of Kristin's classmates, all of them shaking their heads and looking at her pityingly. "After Lipsmacker this whole time, huh, Artiste?" someone whispered.

Kristin felt herself shrink. She quickly turned back to the front of the room and looked down at her desk. *The exam!* It blurred in front of her. *Do not cry. Do not cry. Do not cry*, she told herself. Suddenly, she heard her dad's voice. She was at the fifth-grade soccer championship, and her team was down by one point. There was just a minute left—it was all over, she had thought. "Don't cry, pumpkin," her dad had said. "Not yet. Get your game face on." *Get your game face on, Kristin*, she told herself. She looked down at the test again. "(1) What is $^{40}\!/_{75}$, simplified?" *You know that one, Artiste*, Kristin thought. *You got this. One question at a time.*

The test was a blur. As soon as the bell rang, Kristin practically ran out of class. She couldn't bear having to watch Juan—as he always did after math—pick up his phone and check SocialGram. Unfortunately, in the school's hallways, even her moving at light speed—which was what it felt like—couldn't mask the giggling she heard around her. At her locker, she heard someone ask, "Why would Kristin *paint* Juan? That's so weird."

"Duh, because she's a weirdo," she heard Lisa Rabble-rouser respond. More loudly, she added, "And Juan doesn't like weirdos." Behind her, her posse laughed. Kristin felt her face burning. *I need to escape. There's the door—*

"Hey, Kristin!" a male voice hollered behind her. *Oh no*, Kristin thought. It was Tony Jock, captain of the soccer team, and Juan's best friend! Tony sauntered up to her, standing between her and the door. *And there goes my escape route.* Kristin could barely look at him. "So, I was wondering . . . can I get a painting?"

His friends doubled over laughing while Tony stood there, his expression serious. Kristin stared at him, confused. A few seconds later, Tony started laughing too, as did everyone else watching. Kristin had never wanted so badly to run, to disappear. And yet, in that moment, she could barely move. It felt as if, yet again, she was back in a romantic movie—and everything was in slow motion—but in this movie, there was no happy ending. All she heard was laughing and jeering. All she could imagine was Juan's face, looking at her and laughing. *Kristin, what's wrong with you?* the image asked her. *Why are you so weird?*

"Kristin?"

Kristin's eyes flew open—she hadn't realized she'd shut them—and there, in front of her, was the real Juan. His expression was concerned. Internally, Kristin sighed. *Why is this always happening to me?* The crowd watched them in anticipation. "Now she's really going to get it," Lisa said contentedly to her friends.

"Are you okay?" Juan asked.

Why is he asking me that? He should be disgusted by me. "Um . . . yeah," Kristin stammered. "Listen, I'm so, so sorry about the painting. I didn't even mean to paint it! It was kind of a joke, and I just love to paint . . ."

"Why are you apologizing?" Juan asked. He broke into a smile. "I thought it was super cool."

"What?!" Kristin heard Lisa say indignantly, her smile disappearing. Kristin's heart leaped. *"Cool"? He thinks I'm cool! Well, he thinks the painting is cool. But who cares? Juan Lipsmacker likes my painting!* Behind them, a confused murmur ran through the crowd.

With a perplexed look on his face, Tony stepped out of the crowd. "Dude, what are you doing?" he hissed. "She's so weird. And creepy—who *paints* a picture of someone?" The crowd nodded its assent. "C'mon, man. Let's get out of here." *Great*, Kristin thought. *Goodbye, incredible moment with Juan, and hello, afternoon of despair.*

But Juan didn't move. "Dude, why are you picking on her? Why are you all picking on her?" he said more loudly to the crowd. "She's a crazy-talented artist. Maybe if we all actually got to know her, we would've known that. And at least she doesn't steal photos from other people! *That's* creepy," he continued. Akari, Mila, Ida, and Lisa looked away.

In the corner of the hallway, Kristin's desk partner, Micah Supporter, said, "He's right, guys. Knock it off. And seriously, Kristin, your art is awesome." And just like that, suddenly, everyone was nodding.

"It *was* a really good painting, I guess," Tony said, looking at his feet.

In that moment, Kristin thought of her mom. When Kristin was little, her mom had worked two jobs just to pay the bills. The result? She always looked like a mess—hair astray, her lipstick smudged. At times, Kristin had felt embarrassed for her. "Do you want me to give you a makeover,

Mom?" Kristin asked one day. Her mom had laughed. "Yes, I do! Though," she said thoughtfully, "I don't quite care how anyone sees me. And neither should you! Don't ever let anyone make you feel bad about yourself, Kristin."

With her mom's words echoing in her head, Kristin faced the crowd. "I'm glad you all liked my painting," she said confidently. "It really did seem to make a smack—I mean—splash!" she joked. Everyone laughed. As the crowd dissipated, students came up to Kristin, giving her high fives and telling her how impressed they were by the painting. Out of the corner of her eye, she saw Lisa, Akari, Ida, and Mila slink away disappointedly. *Score one for Artiste*, she thought happily.

"Hey . . . Kristin?" Kristin turned. It was Juan! She'd forgotten he was standing there. *Act cool.*

"Hey!" she said. "Listen . . . thank you so much for that. I have to ask, though . . . why did you do that? Stand up for me?"

Juan shrugged. "It wasn't a big deal," he said. "And it was the right thing to do. Lisa had no right to do that to you. Plus, you're, like, an amazing painter."

Kristin's heart leaped. "Thank you," she said, smiling.

"Anyway . . . I gotta go," he said. "Talk to you later?" Kristin nodded happily.

"Kristin!" Tayshia ran up to her, and the two of them squealed loudly. "That was *amazing*!" Tayshia half yelled. "I'm so glad it all worked out." She gave Kristin a big hug. "And everyone thinks you're super cool now—which means they think I'm cool too!"

Kristin laughed. "I love you, Tay! You're the best best friend!"

Tayshia furrowed her eyebrows, her face turning serious. "Well, if that's true . . ."

"Yeah?" Kristin asked, a little nervously.

Tayshia broke into a big smile. "I want a painting too!"

Kristin grabbed her arm. "C'mon, let's go!" *It's time to paint.*

CHAPTER 5 INTERNET CHALLENGE

Congratulations on completing chapter 5! You're well on your way to becoming an internet upstander.

Kristin Artiste's story is a funny one—filled with mishaps and crushes and a pretty amazing golden retriever—but below the surface, the story spoke to the power of being an upstander. By standing up for Kristin, Juan turned the entire situation around; friends and classmates were soon telling Kristin just how impressed they were by her painting. He likely didn't realize it, but he also did so much more—teaching Kristin confidence, self-belief, and resilience. Juan didn't let the fact that his friends were picking on Kristin deter him; he confronted Tony without escalating the situation. In the end, crisis was averted!

Now that you've finished this chapter and read Kristin's story, it's your turn to be an upstander! Post or share a photo of our custom-made "I am an upstander" graphic on your favorite social media platforms. Include a caption explaining why you choose to be an upstander. "I choose to be an upstander because . . ." See my personalized post below for an example!

Link to upstander graphic:

https://tinyurl.com/rethinkupstander

Trisha's post:

ReThink The Internet

I AM AN
UPSTANDER

Hate has no home on the Internet.

@TrishPrabhu: I've been reading @ReThinktheInternet and have learned so much about spreading kindness, not hate, online. 💕 An important part of that is being an upstander, not a bystander! I'm an upstander because I know what it feels like when no one has your back— and how life-changing even a little support can be. 🌐 #IAmAnUpstander

CHAPTER 6
YOU CAN CHANGE THE WORLD (REALLY!)

Reading this book, you might think the internet is the absolute worst! After all, we've talked about how the internet can bring out the worst in us, and how it's filled with misinformation, deceiving us at every turn. And even if you don't think the internet is a complete mess, you might think I'm an internet-hater (so #uncool). Believe it or not, that couldn't be further from the truth. I actually think technology and the internet are awesome because they can change the world if you use them in the right way. What's "the right way"? There is no one right way! You could use your social media platform to start a movement for justice, learn to code, build an app that helps support the disabled community, conduct science experiments, or more. In my case, I learned to code and built an app that detects and stops cyberbully-ing. Knowing that harassment was a big issue, I decided to take a stand. You can too! No matter what you're passionate about, you should be using tech to support your interests, to be an activist, changemaker, creator, and dreamer. It's sim-ple: with tech and the internet, you can make the world a better place. So embrace tech—to save populations and start revolutions! #GenZStrong 💪

As she walked down the hall, Tanya Techguru could sense she was being watched.

Around her, whispers. Then giggles, followed by cocked eyebrows and shaking heads. "What *is* that thing?" she heard someone whisper.

"Her only friend, apparently," someone else replied, not bothering to lower his voice. Laughter ensued.

"And . . . she *talks* to it?" Tanya heard another girl ask, her voice indignant.

"Uh . . . yeah," the guy replied. "Here's the best part: she named it. I'm not kidding. She calls it Grady or something."

"Ehmagawd," the girl replied, seemingly horrified. "Eww!"

As she made her way to her locker, Tanya sighed. *I'm shocked*, she thought, rolling her eyes. She couldn't believe she'd hoped that fifth grade would be a fresh start, that three months of space from her classmates would mean a chance to start over. "Instead, it looks like it's just you and me again, Grace," she whispered, patting the slim, rectangular box in her hands—her computer. Named after Grace Hopper, a female pioneer in computer science and the person who made the phrase "computer bug" famous, it was Tanya's most prized possession. While most kids went to local electronics stores to buy a computer, Tanya had built hers—just a year before, in the fourth grade! Piece by piece, obsessing over every detail, she'd assembled Grace. The result? An awesome computer . . . that unfortunately didn't quite look like a "normal" computer and put her nerdiness on full display. Tanya knew most fifth graders couldn't have cared less about computer hardware . . . but while most people lived in the "real" world, she lived in a world of 0s and 1s, circuits and processors, coding and creation. Fashion? Makeup? The boy band Three Directions? Tanya couldn't say she was a fan. And it sadly wasn't easy; there wasn't a ton of room in elementary school to be "different"—especially as a girl who loved tech.

As she walked to her first class, Tanya spied the fifth-grade lounge, in all of its glory; complete with a soda cooler, stereo, and snack box, the lounge—open to only the oldest kids in the building—was the highlight of every fifth grader's year. After all, as Class President Asher McLoved had put it, they'd "waited four years for this!" Tanya had hoped to get a glimpse before her classes, but she noticed several people staring at her from inside the lounge, pointing and laughing. Tanya looked down. *Or . . . not. Maybe another time.* Desperate for some quiet, she quickly walked to first-period arts and crafts; in the empty classroom, she took a seat in the back, out of view, and powered on her computer, which whirred to life. Grace's hum settled her; instantly, she felt calmer. *There we go.* She began to set up her work space, moving through each step of her routine. Computer? *Check.* Fancy pens for random bursts of creativity? *Check.* Her "Tanya's Great Ideas" notebook? Still in her bag. She quickly grabbed it. *Check.*

She flipped through the notebook until she finally reached the latest entry, titled "Stay Out!" She smiled. *Ah yes—this might be my best invention yet.* Inspiration had struck the afternoon before, when Tanya was feverishly working through a problem in her code for another one of her projects; just as she'd figured out her mistake, her baby brother, Noam, had come in and raced through her room, destroying her desk space and competition trophies. Tanya had spent thirty minutes cleaning everything up, and by the time she got back to work, she'd forgotten her solution! She knew Noam was only four, so it wasn't really his fault, but enough was enough. Her vision for the "Stay Out" app was simple: it would alert Tanya when motion was sensed outside of her bedroom door, giving her a window of time to catch Noam and lock him in his playroom (far away from her!).

On her computer, Tanya toggled between several windows until she'd pulled up the "Stay Out" application. Inhaling, she cracked her knuckles. "It's time to get to work," she whispered to herself and began to rapidly type.

Tanya's parents had first realized their daughter was—as Tanya's dad put it—a "baby genius" when she was three. As the story went, one afternoon, when toddling around the living room, she'd spied her father's phone on the coffee table. (He'd been busy making lunch and watching soccer—a fact that Tanya's mom liked to remind him of to this day). When he finally brought some lunch over for Tanya, he was in for a surprise: in just ten minutes, she'd completely disassembled his phone, piece by piece—and was examining the circuitry. Horrified, her dad grabbed the phone parts away; in a rush to get everything away from Tanya, he completely missed that his daughter had singlehandedly achieved an incredible feat.

Later that evening, as he and Mrs. Techguru discussed how to get it repaired, Mrs. Techguru realized they'd accidentally left the phone parts on the table again! After rushing into the living room, she was in for a treat: there, on the floor, was Tanya, reassembling the phone. "Mason!" Tanya's mom had yelled. "She's . . . she's . . . fixing the phone!"

"Who is, dear?" Mr. Techguru had called back.

"Our daughter! Tanya!" Astounded, they vowed to help her hone her extraordinary potential.

Fast-forward a few years, and Tanya's penchant for technology had gone far beyond phone repair. At seven, she'd invented the "Scoop-O-Rama," a robot that could form a perfect scoop of ice cream. (And serve it with a "Thank you! Come again!" The Scoop-O-Rama was now in use at the local ice cream parlor, Nomnom's.) At nine, she'd built a "Candy for All" rocket launcher; after liftoff, the mini-rocket

107

had dumped bucket after bucket of candy across town—and even better, the mission went perfectly, with the propeller landing in her backyard just ten minutes after launch. (Unfortunately, the police department arrived soon after. Luckily, Tanya had written a self-destruction routine into the rocket!) No matter the problem—whether achieving the perfect scoop of ice cream or satisfying thousands of sugar-crazed kids—Tanya could build the technology to fix it. And that was what she loved the most about technology: it was so powerful—which meant she was too!

Riiiiiing!

Huh? Tanya looked up, startled. The first bell had rung; the room was now full of students, and at the front of the classroom, Tanya's arts and crafts teacher, Ms. Frigid, had started to explain their lesson that day—on clay pottery. *Hold on*, Tanya thought impatiently. She was so close with this next chunk of code—she just needed one more minute of work time! Unfortunately, Ms. Frigid was *not* computer-friendly. The last time she'd caught Tanya coding during a class, she gave her a one-way ticket to the principal's office. (Of course, it didn't help that Tanya had been building an art simulator to do her homework for her.)

Now Tanya looked between her computer and Ms. Frigid apprehensively. *Wait . . . what was that?* In her line of view, she spotted Andre Petty and Angelo Meeny. They had noticed her working; laughing, Andre grabbed his computer and pretended to kiss it, while Angelo practically fell out of his chair. *Ignore it, Tanya*, she thought. *Remember what Mom*

said—just let it go. You have more important problems to solve.
She refocused on her code; with one eye on Ms. Frigid, she began to surreptitiously type. *Almost there ... Almost there ... Please let this work.* Inhaling, she tested the code chunk. *Yes! It worked!* Tanya felt her heart soar. She was now almost halfway through the app—she'd be done by the end of the week, right on schedule! Nothing was better than the feeling of conquering a new tech challenge. She quickly slid her computer into her bag. *Mission accomplished.*

A second later, Tanya felt a tap on her shoulder. *Crud. Is it ...* Turning, she was pleasantly surprised to see it wasn't Ms. Frigid (thank goodness)—it was Naadir Newsguy, a student in her grade. *Wait, what?* Tanya hadn't talked to Naadir since the second grade. *What does he want?*

"Something's going down! Check your phone," he said, his voice gleeful. "I can't wait to see this," he added under his breath. *Oh great.*

Her heart sinking, Tanya reached into her bag, pretending to grab a notebook; at the last second, she grabbed her phone and took a quick peek at the screen.

1 NEW PICCHAT FROM ANGELO MEENY: Between the haircut and the computer, she's never been so lame. 😂. Why can't u just be a normal girl?

Behind the caption was a picture he'd snapped of Tanya just a few minutes before, bent over her computer, her new pixie haircut on full display. And he'd sent it in the school group PicChat ... so everyone could see, including her.

In that moment, Tanya felt something inside of her

snap. She wasn't sad, confused, or hurt—she was angry. *What does that even mean? That "normal" girls don't love computers? And why the dig at my haircut?* She patted the top of her head self-consciously. When she'd gone in for a haircut a few months prior, she'd noticed another woman with the cut—and it looked awesome. *Why do they care if it's short? More importantly, why do I have to be what they want me to be?* It was so unfair, all of it—the bullying, the mean messages, the constant teasing. And no matter what her mom said, Tanya couldn't "just let it go" anymore. She'd always believed that technology was all-powerful, but it seemed that the one problem she couldn't fix were the mean kids at her school . . . More precisely, the fact that she couldn't seem to find a single friend—just one person—like her. *Is that too much to ask?* If that wasn't an important problem to solve, Tanya didn't know what was.

For the rest of arts and crafts, Tanya was restless; as soon as the bell rang, she grabbed her bag and headed to her free period. She could hear some residual laughter around her—people still looking at the PicChat—but she barely noticed. As soon as she reached the classroom, she immediately set up her workspace again, powering on Grace. She then grabbed her notebook and eagerly flipped to a blank page. At the top of the page, she wrote, with one of her fancy pens, in large block letters:

OPERATION WOMEN RISING

The name was perfect. Now, though, she had to figure out what, exactly, she wanted to build . . . Tanya knew she wanted to create a new community, one that would bring people like her together. *And if there are enough of us, everyone will respect us . . . even Angelo Meeny.* The question was how to actually connect everyone. Over the next hour, Tanya pondered different ideas. Virtual reality glasses? People could put them on and "see" a new reality—one in which women in tech ruled! *Nah . . . It'll be expensive, so a ton of women won't be able to buy them. Next option.* Tanya then started to noodle around in her notebook, sketching anything that came to mind. *Ooh . . . what about an Operation Women Rising conference? We could host it on a social media site, like PicChat.* It was definitely closer, but not quite there. Five iterations later, Tanya still didn't quite have it. She sighed and glanced down at her notebook. To her surprise, a picture stared back at her . . . Had she drawn . . . *a website?* It was a rough outline of what looked like a new social platform. *Wait—that's it! I should build a new kind of social media.* She could call it "Operation Women Rising," or "OWR" for short. It'd be an amazing way for awesome women who loved tech and creation to connect! There'd be only one rule: be kind to everyone. She'd make a ton of friends, Angelo Meeny would be taught a lesson, *and* it was a cool project . . . a win all around.

But it was also going to be a *lot* of work . . . which meant it was time to *get* to work. As the bell rang and Tanya headed off to biology, she had only one thing on her mind: the new website. *It's going to be epic.*

Over the next two weeks, Tanya spent almost every waking moment working on Grace. She started waking up an hour before school (normally, just the thought would make her shudder) to get a head start on that day's milestones. As soon as school let out, she'd race back home and into her kitchen, where she'd scarf down a snack; when she was done, it was straight back up to her room for a marathon of coding, coding, and more coding. Every evening, she'd cross out the parts of the website that she'd finished on her "Operation Women Rising" notebook page.

Unfortunately, working on the website meant even *more* annoying comments at school—her classmates took every opportunity to make fun of her. "Seriously, she's so weird," one of the guys in her Spanish class said. Around him several guys laughed. "She's literally more computer than girl," another guy said. Listening in, Tanya gritted her teeth. *Just you wait, Jonah Annoyme,* she thought. *I'll teach you!* The comments simply added fuel to her fire: they made what she was doing that much more important.

At home, things hadn't started out quite so great, either . . . At first, her parents simply didn't get why she wanted to do the project. When she told her mom about it, Mrs. Techguru had sighed. "I think it's a great idea, Tanya," she'd said. "But . . . I thought you didn't care about what other people thought. What did I tell you about ignoring people like that?"

"Some things just can't be ignored, Mom!" Tanya had argued. "What's the point of being a tech genius if I can't even solve the problems I care about? Or . . . be respected for who I am? Operation Women Rising isn't just about me. It's about . . . changing how people see women. And technology."

Mrs. Techguru had looked at her thoughtfully, her face surprised. "I guess . . . I just don't want you to get hurt, or be bullied even more than I know you are . . . I want to protect you. But you're right, Tanya," she'd said, and nodded. "This is too important not to work on."

Across the kitchen, her dad had nodded. Turning to Mrs. Techguru, he'd said, "Well, will you look at that! Maybe she got the activism from you!" Tanya's mom had been a political organizer and community worker for several years.

I'm . . . an activist, Tanya realized. She'd never seen herself that way, but for the first time, she wanted to be—and was—something more than just a "technology person." *And I really like it.*

A week passed. Several pizzas, early wake-ups, and coding sessions later, Tanya was finally done. As she wrote out the last chunk of code, she felt something inside of her bloom.

```
if (user_status == "logout") {
"Thank you for visiting!"
}
else {
"Thanks for visiting Operation Women Rising. What would you like to check out next?"
}
```

"Done," she whispered, saving her work. She'd really done it! Operation Women Rising was ready to go.

Tanya waited for the usual feeling of triumph to set in, but for some reason, she couldn't shake her nerves; it felt as if there were a pit in the middle of her stomach. *What's wrong with me?* She started to pace in her room, trying to shake the feeling. And yet . . . she was consumed with fear and doubt. *What if people don't like the setup? What if I don't make a single friend?* And perhaps the scariest question: *What if no one joins? What if it's a failure . . . What if I'm a failure?* Tanya had never made something that she cared so much about—in the past, tech creation had always been fun, a way to make something "cool." Now, it was something more serious, something deeper—a way to make something that was important. *It has to be successful.* She didn't know what she'd do otherwise.

For the rest of the evening, Tanya stalled, stress-eating her favorite snack: chocolate-filled marshmallows. (As she often told her mom, sugar was an important part of her creative process! Unfortunately, her mom had yet to buy that.) In front of her, on Grace, was the platform's launch button—with one click, Operation Women Rising would go live on the web. But somehow, Tanya just couldn't bring herself to do it—she was still too afraid. *In fact,* she thought as she swiveled away from Grace, *I think it's time to go grab some more marshmallows.* Downstairs, as she passed the refrigerator in her kitchen, a new picture stuck to the steel exterior caught her eye. *I've never seen that before. Is that . . . ?*—she slowly approached the photo—*It is!* It was her mom, back when she was in high school. *She looks so different.* In the picture, her mom was wearing an oversize pink T-shirt with the word FEMINIST across it and holding a large sign: "Women's rights are human rights. We are unafraid!"

Staring at the sign, Tanya felt something inside of her stir. *Activists are unafraid.* If she really wanted to be an activist, she realized, she needed to take a chance, a leap of faith. She was reminded of a quote that Grace Hopper had loved, which had also become her favorite: "A ship in port is safe, but that is not what ships are built for." *I need to sail out to sea and do things.* Marshmallows forgotten, Tanya ran back up to her room. Mustering her courage, with her eyes squeezed half shut, she nervously reached out to Grace—and pressed LAUNCH.

The platform was live! Her eyes wide, Tanya refreshed the web page, over and over again. *Are people joining?* She'd put advertisements in all of her favorite technology newsletters and PicChat groups, and she'd gotten a ton of likes! *Please join*, she prayed quietly. Trying to ignore the worry brewing inside of her, she stayed by Grace for the rest of the evening, waiting for the *buzz* that would tell her someone—even a single, solitary person—had signed up. But three hours later . . . she was still at zero users.

Exhausted and heartbroken, Tanya collapsed onto her bed. *I'm so tired. And defeated. At least tomorrow's a Saturday.* Not bothering to change out of her lucky sweater—which, it turned out, was not so lucky after all—she crawled under her bed covers and quickly fell asleep.

Buzz. Buzz. Buzz.

Tanya awoke the next morning to the sound of notifications on Grace. Groggy, she squinted at the sunlight filling her room, confused. *What is that?* As soon as she'd reoriented, she remembered last night's failure: *how humiliating.* The one upside? She planned to spend the day in bed, watching *Computing: A Historical Documentary* and eating popcorn. If there was anyone who deserved a pity party, it was her . . . *Buzz. Buzz.* Tanya sighed. *Why is Grace doing that? Unless . . .* "Let me guess. It's another love letter from Angelo Meeny and the rest of the school," she whispered to herself sarcastically. Steeling herself, she grabbed Grace off her desk and roused her from sleep mode.

Immediately, the Operation Women Rising platform appeared. And that's when she saw it: Operation Women Rising . . . had one thousand new users?! Tanya blinked several times; was she reading that correctly? Was it a bug in the code? Had they been hacked? Unable to believe it, she quickly navigated to the platform's home page, where she'd included a public map of all of Operation Women Rising's users—*Oh. My. Gosh. It not a mistake!* Tanya had hoped for 100 people—at most—to join Operation Women Rising in its first week . . . The latest tally put the platform at—*buzz*—now 1,001 users in just twelve hours! *And they're from all over!* There were even fifteen users from Asia. Tanya was shocked—Operation Women Rising wasn't a failure; it was a *massive* success.

Tanya's heart leaped. "I guess you do still have it," she whispered happily to her lucky sweater. Joyous, she started to dance on top of her bed, jumping up and down to silent music. *I did it, I did it, oh yeah, yeah, yeah; I did it, I did it—*

The door to her bedroom opened. It was her mom. Tanya abruptly stopped, mid-dance. "Uh . . . hey," she said, red-faced, dropping and casually reclining onto her bed.

"Well, hello there," Mrs. Techguru said, and laughed. "I'm glad to see you're in such a good mood this morning. Just coming in for your laundry." Smiling, she quickly closed the door behind her. Normally, Tanya would've died of embarrassment . . . but today, she couldn't have cared less. Operation Women Rising was a success! Nothing else really mattered.

As the feeling of excitement finally receded, Tanya glanced back at Grace. *One thousand (and one!) followers. I wonder who they all are* . . . Curious, she grabbed Grace and opened her up again.

On Operation Women Rising, she clicked on the Women Rising feed. Immediately, hundreds of posts began to appear. Reading through them, Tanya was stunned—not only were these women so cool, so many of them loved exactly the same things as Tanya (including chocolate-filled marshmallows!). And, honestly speaking, they were even more talented than she was (even if that was a little hard to admit). Take Karishma Hotshot (@Karish), from California. **Hi, y'all! I'm Karishma H. I'm 14 years old, and I'm currently building a self-driving car. I love coding and robots, and, of course,**

junk food! Excited to meet y'all! ❤. Tanya smiled and liked Karishma's post. *That's so cool.*

A second later, a message appeared in Tanya's Operation Women Rising MessageBox—from Karishma! Tanya eagerly clicked on it.

@Karish: Hey hey hey!! OWR is SO cool. Amazing job. I'm Karishma by the way!

Tanya beamed. Someone had called her . . . *cool*. That definitely wasn't something she heard every day!

@Tanya_TechGoddess: Omg hi! Thank you SO much. Welcome to OWR!

@Karish: Btw do you mind if I share this on my PicChat? I have a ton of followers so I think I could get more ppl to join!

@Tanya_TechGoddess: That would be AMAZING yes pls do

What was "a ton of followers"? Tanya grabbed her phone, opened PicChat, and typed in Karishma's name. The profile immediately popped up— *Whoa*. Tanya's jaw dropped. *Hold up. Three MILLION followers?!* That's when Tanya realized—Karishma Hotshot was the famous actor Hottie Hotshot's daughter! Hottie had starred in only every famous movie ever (he had three Moscars!) . . . and now his daughter was using Operation Women Rising! *The platform I built!* Suddenly, Tanya thought of Angelo Meeny. *If only he could see me now!* She didn't just have friends—she was friends with *the* Karishma Hotshot.

Speaking of Angelo . . . Tanya quickly checked Karishma's followers on PicChat. Sure enough, there it was . . .

@COOLANGELOMEENY FOLLOWS KARISHMA! *Perfect*, Tanya thought. He was about to learn a lesson: *don't mess with Tanya Techguru!*

Later that day—after hours spent on Operation Women Rising—Tanya relayed the entire story to her parents. "And, y'all, as of"—Tanya quickly peeked at Grace—"three-oh-five p.m. today . . . Operation Women Rising has . . . wait for it . . . fifty thousand users!" Thanks to Karishma's post, the platform had gone viral. She still couldn't wrap her head around it. "It's definitely the best thing I've ever built," she said. *And not just because it has been so successful—the women on the platform are truly the best.* Tanya had finally found a group—her group.

"That's absolutely amazing, sweetheart," Mr. Techguru said. Next to Tanya, Mrs. Techguru nodded. "I'm so proud of you . . . especially because, well . . . I was wrong, and you figured that out," she said solemnly. A second later, she mock-sighed. "And that is why I like your brother more . . ." They all laughed together.

"Well, I have to head out—I'm going to a rally—but I'll see you for dinner," Mrs. Techguru said as she grabbed her purse. About to head back upstairs, Tanya suddenly stopped. *Wait—a rally?* Normally, she wouldn't really care, but for some reason, today, her interest was piqued. "What rally, Mom?"

"For Which It Stands is trying to raise funds for the

town's homeless population," Mrs. Techguru explained. For Which It Stands was the nonprofit organization Tanya's mom worked for. "We're hoping that the rally gets enough attention—and gets people to spend more." She sighed. "It's just so hard to keep them giving afterward. If they can't 'see' the issue, they don't care," she said, exasperated. "Of course, the need is still there."

Tanya frowned. *There has to be a better way.* And that's when . . . *I have a great idea.* "Wait!" Tanya yelled out. Mrs. Techguru looked up at her, startled. "What if I helped build something? To help with the donations? It could be a platform that shares some of the homeless folks' stories, or even includes a dashboard of how the dollars are being spent."

Mrs. Techguru's eyes lit up. "Tanya! That's . . . an amazing idea," she said. "How did I not think of that before?"

"I'll take that as a yes," Tanya said, and smiled. "So . . . I guess I'll come to the rally with you, then. Let me just grab my coat—and Grace!"

"Hold on," Mrs. Techguru sounded confused. "You *want* to come to the rally?"

"I'm an activist, right?" Tanya replied.

There was a small pause—after which Mrs. Techguru grinned broadly. "That you are, Tanya." They high-fived. "Okay, okay . . . enough talk," Mrs. Techguru said. "It's time for action. Let's go!"

Tanya ran to the front door. *Let's do this thing, Grace,* she thought, glancing down at her computer. Together, they were all-powerful—and ready to use that power for good.

CHAPTER 6 INTERNET CHALLENGE

Congratulations on completing chapter 6! Whether you're a budding activist, creator, or explorer, you're one step closer to making change.

You might not have a genius IQ, but you probably have a talent or an interest—something you're passionate about. As we read in chapter 6, in Tanya's case, that passion is creation—and using technology, she builds some seriously awesome stuff, from the candy rocket to the art homework simulator. Between the laughs, though, were important lessons: Tanya's decision to build Operation Women Rising, for example, stemmed from her frustration with the gender bias and taunting she encountered at school. Angelo Meeny wasn't just mean—he thought technology isn't for girls! Tanya definitely proved him wrong, and along the way, discovered that **tech creation can be more than just a hobby: it can make the world a better place**. Indeed, as she put her plan for Operation Women Rising into action, Tanya discovered her love of activism, and a deep desire to make change. As we saw, technology was an incredible vehicle for that.

Now that you've finished the chapter and read Tanya's story, it's time to get your start on being a technology-powered changemaker. Brainstorm a way you can use technology to support your interests—and those around you—and put it into action. It can be as simple as starting an online fundraiser for a local sports team or making a video for your mom on Mother's Day. There's only one rule: show the world the power of using technology for good. Use the hashtag "#TechForGood" when you share your efforts on social media!

CHAPTER 7
#IRL

I f I wanted to, I could spend all day on my phone. (And . . .
if I'm being honest, sometimes, it feels like I do! 😄) After
all, there are so many TikTok dances to master (Renegade!),
games to play, and friends to text. (And what's a good friend
if they don't immediately respond with their opinion on my
life crises?) So it's totally justified if you're wondering, *Really,
what's wrong with spending a bunch of time on my phone?*
Well . . . for one, being on your phone all the time isn't good
for you. Science says that people who spend a ton of time
on their phones may actually be less happy (which no one
wants!), and using your phone too much can even make it
more difficult for you to fall asleep (if you're all about the
#NapGame, like I am, that can be a serious problem). But
even worse, too much time on your phone can mean that it

starts to replace your life. Technology is great when it enhances your life—makes everything in your life, like your friendships and interests, even better. Being able to text a friend when you need to is the best—but spend too much time on your phone, and soon *all* you'll do is text your friend (instead of spend time with them—which is what a friendship really needs). That's exactly what happened to me the summer before seventh grade: My best friend and I finally got phones and started texting each other all the time. But we didn't really make time to hang out or do all the things we used to love to do (watch movies, chat crushes, and eat way too much ice cream). When the school year started, it was like we didn't know each other . . . and it was the worst. Take it from me: don't let your phone take over your life—be thoughtful about the time you spend on your phone (or any device).

Calvin McBestie wiped the sticky sweat dripping off his face. *Nasty.* Mid-court, he paused to catch his breath. He was exhausted—physically and mentally. *Pull yourself together*, he thought. *This is it.* Above him, the court's timer read, in big block letters, 0:15. *There's just fifteen seconds left in the game.* He glanced at the scoreboard. Blueridge Fancy Pants—91; Woodlawn Troopers—90. *This is the Troopers'—my—last chance.* The audience buzzed with excitement; out of the corner of his eye, he could see his mom cheering from the bleachers. She was holding a sign: "Let's GO Troopers Basketball!"

Calvin heard the ref blow his whistle; a second later, his teammate, Tyrone Friend, passed the ball to the Troopers point guard—his best friend, Paul Fonelover. Immediately, the timer started to count down. Paul rapidly advanced the ball up the court; at the free-throw line, he paused, and moved to take the shot. The audience watched, breathless. But then . . . suddenly, Paul locked eyes with Calvin. Calvin smiled. *I know that look.* A second later, Paul faked a shot—sending the Fancy Pants defensive player in the wrong direction—and in one motion, passed the ball to Calvin. *It's all me now.* As the audience roared, Calvin pivoted back, exhaled, and sent the ball flying toward the net. In that moment, everything seemed to slow—and as the ball hurtled toward the basket, Calvin felt himself hoping, praying . . . *Please let it go in.*

And then— *Whoosh.* He made the shot! "Nothing but net!" someone in the crowd hollered. As the bleachers erupted, Calvin heard the buzzer sound. He'd done it—*the Troopers won!* A second later, his teammates were all over him, chanting his name. "Let's go, dude!" Tyrone yelled, slapping his back. They all started to laugh and cheer. Four months of grueling practice made the win that much sweeter.

Calvin found himself looking for someone— *There he is.* Paul! They ran toward each other until they collided midcourt, and began to jump up and down. "You *did* the thing, dude!" he heard Paul yell. "That's my boy!" Mid-jump,

Calvin yelled back, "It was all you. You're the master!"

"Good evening, boys," Calvin heard someone say. They both abruptly stopped jumping. To their left stood an eager-looking middle-aged woman holding a large notepad. Behind her stood a camera crew. "My name is Avayah Sentinel, and I'm here with the Woodlawn News team. We'd love to feature you in a segment that'll be airing tomorrow morning. Do you have a minute?"

Calvin hesitated—he'd always been one to shy away from any attention—but Paul grabbed him, planting him directly in front of the camera. "Absolutely!" Paul said, and smiled. "We'd love to, right, Calvin?" he said, slapping Calvin's back. *Great*, Calvin thought as he shrugged.

"Wonderful! My first question is . . ." Ms. Sentinel consulted her notebook. "Tell me about that last shot . . . take me through those fifteen seconds; how did you two work together to execute that play? Had you practiced it before? It looked like it took exceptional teamwork." She extended the mic to Calvin.

"Uh . . ." Calvin spluttered. He could feel himself turning red. *Think, Calvin; just say something!* "Uh . . ."

Suddenly, Paul grabbed the microphone. "Well, I guess it's my turn to assist!" he joked. Calvin smiled and ducked his head. *This is why Paul and I work so well—Paul always has my back . . . and has a big mouth.* "It's really simple," Paul continued, waving his hands energetically. "Calvin's my best friend—and that gives us a huge advantage on the court, because we're able to read each other. We'd actually never practiced that play before," he said, glancing at Calvin, who nodded. "But basketball is all about teamwork and coordination. And we won tonight because we have the best team!" Around them, some fans cheered. *Mark my words*, Calvin thought. *Someday, Paul is going to be the mayor of Woodlawn.*

"Cut!" Ms. Sentinel yelled. "That . . . was . . . perfect! You are incredible!" she said, looking directly at Paul.

Paul smiled. "I think you mean . . . we're both incredible," he said, cocking his head.

Burn! Calvin thought.

Ms. Sentinel gasped. "Oh . . . yes, yes! Of course! That's what I meant."

Paul smiled sweetly at her reaction. "Well, then . . . c'mon, Calvin!" As they ran back to the lockers, they both started to laugh. *Calvin and Paul: 1. Avayah Sentinel: 0.*

For as long as Calvin could remember, he'd done pretty much everything with his best friend—with Paul. They'd met in the first grade, when they'd bonded over how much they hated their reading teacher, Mrs. Stickler. Naturally, they booby-trapped her classroom on the last day of the school year—and one school suspension later, as Paul put it, "a beautiful friendship was born."

Most people at school jokingly called them "Palvin" because it was so rare to see one without the other. They were neighbors, took the same seventh-grade classes, were both on Woodlawn Middle School's varsity basketball team, and played in the marching band (both on trumpet). And on the weekends, you could usually find them at VideoWorld, the local video game store, where they'd compete for hours in tournaments (their team name was Palvin, of course!).

This basketball win was just the latest in a string of Palvin accomplishments! Which is why Calvin was in such a great mood when his mom dropped him off at Woodlawn Middle School the Monday after the big game. It was the day of the celebratory pep rally, when the whole school would gather for the hoisting of the division trophy. Coincidentally, it was also Paul's birthday—so, as he'd put it, "double the celebration!" Calvin immediately headed for the C-wing, where Paul, Tyrone, and their other teammates usually hung out before the first bell. When he arrived, he saw Tyrone and their other friend, Ramón, but no Paul. *Hmph. He'd usually be here, especially on his birthday.* "Hey, have you seen Paul?" he asked Tyrone. Tyrone shook his head. "Nah, man. But, dude . . . we have *got* to talk about that play y'all pulled off on Friday!"

In first-period biology, Calvin noticed that Paul was absent. *Weird . . .* It was only at the end of the period that Paul finally sauntered in, to applause and cheers from the class. "Let's go, Troopers!" Ramón yelled.

Ms. Hardheart, their teacher, crossed her arms, displeased. "Congratulations on your win, Mr. Fonelover. Unfortunately, that doesn't excuse you from class."

Paul smiled—as always—sweetly. "I have a pass, Ms.

Hardheart," he said, extending it to her. She grabbed it from him and narrowed her eyes.

"Take a seat," she said sharply.

"Dude! Happy birthday!" Calvin exclaimed as Paul settled in next to him. "Also . . . I didn't think Ms. Hardheart could hate you more." They both laughed. "Why are you late? What were you doing?"

Paul grinned. "As a birthday gift, my parents let me play hooky . . . to have breakfast at the Pancake House," he said while Calvin groaned in jealousy. The Pancake House had *the best* pancakes. Just thinking about the Triple Chocolate Delight made Calvin woozy.

"Oh man!" Calvin said. "You're so lucky." *His* mom had yelled at him for being late to breakfast (of course).

Paul glanced surreptitiously at Ms. Hardheart. "And it only gets better, dude! They also got me . . ." He reached into his backpack and slyly pulled something out. Calvin squinted. *Wait, what is that?* "A phone! Finally, man!" Paul said, waving it.

Internally, Calvin was stunned—and felt a sharp pang of jealousy. *A cell phone? Paul got a cell phone?* Calvin had been begging his mom to get him a phone for years—but she had decreed that he "wasn't ready yet." And this was when almost everyone else in their grade already had a phone. Up to that point, it hadn't been the worst thing, especially because Paul didn't have one . . . But now he did! *How is that fair?* Calvin knew he should've been happy for his friend, but he couldn't help it. This majorly sucked.

To make matters worse, Paul barely noticed—he was . . . too busy looking at his new phone! "Dude, look at this thing—it's so sick! I can text, like, anyone I want, like Ramón and Tyrone. And I've already downloaded so many games, including Fortress Dynamite!"

Calvin looked up suddenly. *Oh no . . . please don't tell me.* Fortress Dynamite was their favorite VideoWorld video game. "You can . . . play Fortress Dynamite on your phone?" he said, his voice uncertain.

"Yeah, man!" Paul nodded enthusiastically. "They match you with random players. And honestly"—he lowered his voice—"it totally beats VideoWorld. It's the best." His voice trailed off as he checked a text. Calvin sighed deeply, worry bubbling inside of him. Why did it feel like all of a sudden everything was changing? *Because it is*, a voice inside his head said. *Paul is going to be playing Fortress Dynamite without you. Soon enough, he'll be hanging out with Ramón and Tyrone—not you.*

Shut up! Calvin thought.

"Dude? Hello?" Calvin blinked. Paul was staring at him. "Earth to Calvin," he said, moving a hand in front of his face. "Come in, Calvin." Calvin smiled faintly. "What's wrong, bro?" Paul asked, his voice curious.

"Nothing!" Calvin said, shrugging. "Why would something be wrong?"

Paul clucked his tongue. "Ah—is this because your mom won't get you one? A phone, I mean?" Calvin looked away. "Dude, it's just a phone. It's not a big deal. Besides, you can use this!" Paul said emphatically. *Huh?* Calvin was bewildered. *What on earth is he talking about?* Paul explained: "Tell your mom that I got a phone, and then she'll get you one too. This is your chance!"

Wait a second. Calvin hadn't thought about it that way . . . Now things didn't seem so bad. If this ended up working out for him, it could be a win all around. *Yeah . . . I'll tell her that Paul got one, and then she'll realize that I need one too. Maybe Mrs. Fonelover can help convince her!* Suddenly, Calvin was in a great mood again. For the rest of the day, he imagined his mom finally admitting he deserved a phone. He'd play Fortress Dynamite with Calvin every day during biology! *It's going to be awesome. Calvin and Paul: 1. The Phone: 0.*

"No, Calvin. For the hundredth time, the answer is no. That's final." Calvin's mom shook her head firmly and walked back into the kitchen.

On the couch in the living room, Calvin sunk into the plush cushions. *What?* A second later, he sprung up again, trailing her. "Mom! C'mon," he said, his voice urgent. "You don't understand— I need this. If I don't get a phone, soon I'm going to be the *only* person in the grade without one. Do you really want that for me? And . . . if Mrs. Fonelover thinks Paul is ready, why don't you think I'm ready?" he asked.

Calvin's mom sighed. "Frankly, I don't know that I agree with Mr. and Mrs. Fonelover's decision. But that's out of my hands. This"—she gestured around the room—"is not. This is my house. My house, my rules—conversation over." Calvin looked away. "Now grab a dish towel, and come help with these dishes." *Could she make me hate her any more?*

After a wordless dinner, Calvin returned to his room, angry and frustrated. Did his mom want him to be the lamest kid in the school? *Because that's what she's setting me up to be.* He tried to do his biology homework but couldn't focus. All he could think about was Paul, his mom, and the injustice of it all . . . The worst part was, there was nothing he could do about it.

After an hour of stewing, he hadn't made any progress on his homework . . . and the sun was starting to set. *Forget this.* Calvin shoved the homework into his backpack. When was he ever going to need to know about animal cell structure, anyway? He wanted to do the only thing that ever calmed him down: shoot some hoops. He headed out ("Yes, Mom, I finished all of my homework!" he lied) and over to Paul's house. He knew Paul would be free to get a few baskets up— and take Calvin's mind off things.

Paul's mom opened the door and smiled broadly. "Hey, Calvin! Congratulations again on the big game! How are you?"

Calvin smiled. "Thanks, Mrs. Fonelover. I'm good. I wanted to see if Paul was around? I was thinking we could play a little ball."

"Oh . . ." Mrs. Fonelover pursed her lips. "Paul is on the phone with a friend right now, so I don't think he's free. But maybe tomorrow?"

Of course. Despite the anger building in his chest, Calvin forced a smile. "Yeah . . . of course. Thanks, Mrs. Fonelover. Have a good evening." On the way back to his house, Calvin kicked a rock in fury, stubbing his toe; he limped the rest of the way, and then up the stairs, collapsing onto his bed. His foot looked swollen and red. *Oops . . . Coach BeBall is not going to be pleased.* In his defense, it had been the worst day ever—far from a victory lap. *Please let tomorrow be better.* Exhausted and drained, Calvin immediately fell asleep.

Unfortunately, the next morning Calvin quickly learned his wish had *not* come true: thanks to his rock-kicking episode, he'd been rendered useless on the basketball court. Staring at his foot, Coach BeBall sighed. "What on earth did you do, McBestie? I thought we made it clear that your physical health was of the utmost importance. You need to be on the court, preparing for next season!" He shook his head. "Okay. Okay. Fine. Static practice only today. You'll be shooting free throws with Fonelover; he can grab the ball and pass it back to you so you don't have to move around. Speaking of which . . ." He looked up and down the gym. "Where *is* that kid?"

Calvin had no idea; Paul was usually never late to practice. Calvin was mystified . . . and honestly, kind of worried. *What if something happened? What if it's something serious?* He knew what he had to do: the thing he'd tried to avoid doing all morning. "Hey, Ramón!" he yelled across the court. Ramón looked up. Calvin sighed. *Here goes.* "Do you know where Paul is? I mean, like, have y'all been texting?"

Ramón laughed. "Yeah, dude! My man was texting Yuja Cutie last night. You know—the really nice girl in our English class? He was up until eleven p.m. He liiikes her!" he said, his voice teasing. "So . . . if I had to guess, he probably didn't set an alarm."

Calvin couldn't believe it. *No way! Paul is getting girls now? And all it took was the stupid phone?!* More importantly, why hadn't Paul mentioned anything? Calvin didn't really know how to feel . . . except that he hated this, all of it.

As if on cue, the door to the gym opened, and Paul flew in. Next to Calvin, Coach BeBall jumped up. "Fonelover! In my office now!" he screamed angrily. "What is it with my star players today?" he muttered to himself, glancing at Calvin, who looked down.

For the rest of the day, Calvin tried to catch a moment with Paul, but it never seemed to happen. He wasn't in their usual hangout spots, he arrived late to every class, and he left every class as soon as the bell rang ("Sorry, dude, I gotta hit the restroom"). After school, he said he had to skip band practice. "Wait, why?" Calvin asked, his brows furrowed.

"Oh . . . uh." Paul seemed uncertain. "I'm not feeling super well, I guess."

Oh. Suddenly, Calvin felt bad. "That sucks, man," he said. "Sorry, dude."

"It's no biggie." Paul shrugged. "I'll . . . get over it, you know?"

"Yeah," Calvin said. "So . . . um . . . do you want to shoot around the ball tonight?"

Buzz. Paul reached into his pocket and pulled out his phone. His face lit up, and he started to laugh. "Oh, man! Ramón just crushed another level on Fortress Dynamite!" Glancing back at Calvin, he started, as if he'd forgotten his friend was standing there. "Sorry, dude, what was that?" he asked, his eyes still on his phone.

Calvin looked down. "I, uh . . . asked if you wanted to shoot around the basketball."

"Um . . ." Paul hesitated. "I mean, I can, if you want, but . . . you know, I might not be feeling well, right?"

Duh, Calvin thought. "Of course!" he said. "Sorry, dude. Feel better." He patted Paul on the back.

"Thanks, man! I'll talk to you later," Paul said. A second later, he was gone.

As he walked to band practice, Calvin took a few deep breaths. On the one hand, that had kinda sucked. *I was really hoping to shoot some baskets tonight—and hang out with Paul.* But on the other hand . . . maybe he was totally blowing things out of proportion. After all, Paul was sick; maybe *that* was why he'd been all over the place today. And even if it wasn't, Calvin couldn't really blame Paul for being excited by his new phone; Calvin knew he would've been stoked if he'd gotten a new phone. Plus, what was he really worried about? They'd been bros forever. A phone couldn't—and wouldn't— change that. *Just take a chill pill, Calvin. Stop being so . . . clingy.* By the time he got home that evening, Calvin had resolved to just let the whole thing go. *I'll just forget about all of this. Calvin and Paul: 0. The Phone: 1.*

And so, for the rest of the week, Calvin tried his hardest to just "be cool." When Paul skipped lunch on Wednesday and Thursday, leaving Calvin alone in the cafeteria, he brushed it off. *Maybe he's busy with homework.* And when Paul said he still wasn't feeling super well, Calvin invited Ramón over to shoot around the basketball. (The guys on the team were stunned. "You were playing . . . *without* Paul?" Tyrone asked mock-incredulously as Calvin swatted him over the head.) And on Friday, when Paul—who'd missed basketball practice again that morning, leaving Calvin without a partner—rushed into biology and begged to copy Calvin's homework answers, he'd let him. "So the big man can't do his homework now, huh?" Calvin had asked jokingly. Paul had rolled his eyes and laughed . . . but said nothing. Each blow sucked—but Calvin didn't want to be a crybaby. *So what? It's not a big deal*, he told himself. *Let it go.*

Internally, Calvin was so excited for the weekend: no matter what was happening, ever, Calvin and Paul *always* spent the weekend at VideoWorld. Fortress Dynamite 2 was out, and Palvin had another tournament to conquer! Yes, they hadn't gotten any practice in this week . . . but they were unbeatable; that was just a fact of nature. Calvin couldn't wait to destroy the other teams (all while gorging on fried mozz sticks and pepperoni pizza—delish).

At the end of the day, Calvin met Paul at his locker. "Hey! So I'll see you at seven?" Paul looked up from his phone, confused. "Huh? What are you talking about?"

"Nice try," Calvin said, smiling. "But I'm not falling for that. Also, I was thinking about our strategy for the fifth level, when they release the fire-breathing dragons—"

"Oh . . . you mean the FD2 tournament?" Paul asked. *Wait—has he actually forgotten?* "Um, about that—I can't go, actually," he said, almost nervously.

Calvin's jaw dropped. "What?! No, no, no," he moaned. "Dude! But, like, we *never* miss a tournament, ever. And if we win this one, we'll beat VideoWorld's tournament record! This is our chance, man!"

Paul sighed. "I know, I know . . . but . . ." He seemed to be searching for words. "My . . . mom isn't feeling super well, so I need to watch my little sister."

Argh. That sucks. "Sorry, dude. That's super annoying," Calvin said. He sincerely felt bad; he couldn't imagine having to miss FD2 to watch a toddler! "Why didn't you mention it, though?" he asked, confused.

Paul shrugged. "Just fell off my radar, I guess. But yeah, it's super annoying. Sorry, man."

Even though he understood, when Calvin got home that afternoon, he was still really disappointed. He also felt bad for Paul—he had been so excited about FD2! *Oh well.* Moping around the house, Calvin settled on the couch, idly flipping through TV channels; he had just about resigned himself to an evening of watching the GamerWorld channel when his mom walked into the kitchen. She shrieked loudly, dropping the bags in her arms; groceries flew everywhere.

"Mom!" Calvin stood up. "What are you doing?" he asked, staring at the mess.

His mom put her hand over her chest, breathing loudly. "I could ask you the same thing! What are you doing here?" she spluttered. "You're never home on Friday evenings; you and Paul are always at . . . what's that place? VideoWorld! You half scared me to death. I thought you were an intruder!"

After Calvin explained, his mom shook her head. "Well, I'm sorry to hear Mrs. Fonelover isn't well! We should bring a basket over. Actually," she said, glancing at the groceries that had missed the floor, "I think I have enough here to put together our traditional McBestie basket. Can you take it over? I'm sure Paul would appreciate seeing you, even for a little." Calvin perked up: that was actually a pretty good idea. *It would definitely make for a less boring evening.*

After dinner, Calvin headed over to the Fonelovers', basket in hand. It was overflowing; Calvin's mom had stuffed it full with jam, bread, desserts, and flowers. And Calvin had walked over to the local grocery store to buy Paul's favorite snack—Goldfish—which he put right on top.

He knocked on the door; a second later, it swung open. It was Mrs. Fonelover. "Hi, Calvin! Oh my! Wow—what's that?" *For someone who isn't feeling well, she doesn't look that bad*, Calvin thought curiously. She was wearing a bright pink shirt, splattered with flour and sugar. "I'm making a chocolate cake," she explained.

Huh. Not your typical R&R activity, but okay, then . . . "Nice!" Calvin said awkwardly. "Well . . . my family and I wanted to bring this over. Get well soon!" He extended the basket.

Mrs. Fonelover looked confused. "'Get well'? What do you mean?"

Now Calvin was confused. "Uh . . . I mean, like, feel better soon! Paul mentioned you weren't feeling too well, and we just thought we'd share a basket."

Mrs. Fonelover shook her head. "Oh dear . . . well, this is very kind of you all, but there must have been some kind of mistake—I'm doing just fine," she said, her voice bright. "I'm not sure why Paul would say that—maybe you misheard? But this was, uh, touching. Very kind of you both; thank you."

Calvin was shocked. *Wait . . . what? This could only mean one thing: Paul lied to me! Why would he do that?* Calvin didn't know, but he was so angry he could barely think. *When I find Paul Fonelover, he's going to get a piece of me.* He was done letting it go. Paul was being a jerk, and it wasn't okay. Calvin was so furious, he forgot that he was still standing at the door. He quickly looked back up at Mrs. Fonelover, who was staring at him as if he were a crazy person! "Are you okay, dear?" she asked, her voice concerned. "You're looking a little pale. Maybe you're not well? Should I call your mother?"

"No!" Calvin forced a smile. "That won't be necessary, Mrs. Fonelover; I'm great. Actually . . . do you happen to know . . . where Paul is?"

Mrs. Fonelover nodded. "Oh yes! In his room. Do you

want to go on up? I'm sure Paul will love the Goldfish." *Oh, that's not the only thing coming his way,* Calvin thought.

A minute later, Calvin burst into Paul's room. He'd expected to see a lot of things: Maybe Paul and Ramón, hanging out without him? Or Paul and Yuja Cutie, on a date that he'd never told Calvin about? Instead, Paul was lying on his bed . . . on his phone? *What? Wait . . . is that . . . ?* It was— the theme music for Fortress Dynamite 2! Paul was playing Fortress Dynamite 2—without him! Calvin couldn't believe it: Paul had traded time with him for time with his phone, doing the *exact same thing.*

Paul quickly sat up, his eyes wide. "Hey, dude," he said casually. "What's up?" Calvin crossed his arms, wordless. Paul quickly backtracked. "Okay, okay . . . Listen, I wasn't super honest earlier today—"

"Yeah, I know!" Calvin yelled, his anger boiling over. "Your *mom* just told me!" Paul looked away. "What happened to hanging out together? Being best friends? Having each other's backs? Or does your phone do that for you now?" Calvin asked bitterly.

Paul looked guilty. "I know . . . and I'm sorry, man," he said. "Really. I just . . . kind of got used to playing FD2 on my phone, you know? And VideoWorld just seemed, I don't know . . . a little boring?" Calvin opened his mouth, furious, but Paul quickly kept talking: "But it wasn't cool! And I didn't mean to lie to you; it just came out. I've felt bad about it all evening."

"Well, I'm sorry VideoWorld has suddenly become 'boring,' but that's all I can do, at least for now," Calvin shot back. "Part of having someone's back is being there for them, even when it's not convenient for you." That was one of Coach BeBall's basketball mantras; Calvin knew Paul recognized it, because he sighed. "And you know it's not boring!" Calvin pressed, frustrated. "You just want to be on your phone, twenty-four seven!"

The room was silent. When he finally spoke, Paul's voice was sad. "Okay. You know what? You're right . . . I'm kinda addicted to my phone. And no, it's not okay." He seemed genuinely regretful. "I'm really sorry that I let it get in the way of our friendship. I didn't realize how much this has sucked for you." *Finally!* Calvin thought. Paul continued: "I promise—I'm not going to do this again, okay? I won't spend all my time on this." He waved his phone in the air. "And I won't lie to you. So . . . uh . . . do you forgive me?"

There was a pause. Out of the corner of his eye, Calvin saw Paul's basketball from the championship game sitting on his desk. He walked over and passed it to Paul, who caught it, surprised. "Wanna shoot some hoops?" Calvin asked.

Paul slowly grinned. "Yeah, man. Let's do it!" He dropped his phone on his bed, and they raced out of the house. As he shot the ball into the air, Calvin felt himself relax. *My best friend is back—and so is our winning streak.*

Calvin and Paul: 1. The World: 0.

CHAPTER 7 INTERNET CHALLENGE

Congratulations on completing chapter 7! You're well on your way to mastering the art of screen time.

As we learned in chapter 7, screen time can be tricky! Calvin and Paul were close friends—the kind of friends who can't imagine anything coming between them—until, of course, Paul gets his new phone. While Calvin is left hanging (and disappointed that he doesn't have one!), Paul doesn't realize the extent to which he's alienating his friend—until suddenly, he's, in Calvin's words, "being a jerk": always too busy on his phone to have an actual conversation, skipping basketball practice, and even lying to his friend. Rather than enhancing his life, Paul's phone starts to replace it. By the time the situation reaches a tipping point, Paul's new phone has done plenty of damage. It was only by remembering what really matters—the people in his life, including his best friend—that Paul was able to get back on track.

Now that you've read Calvin and Paul's story, it's time to find out just how much time you spend on your phone! Tomorrow, record the time that you pick up your phone, and then the time you put it down. Also note what you did on your phone—did you text someone? Go on social media? Check your email? (Your phone may actually do this for you! See the short note below to help you figure out if it does.) At the end of the day, have a friend add up all of the time (no cheating!) to determine just how much time you're spending on your device.

POST?

Then complete the following exercise:

i. Where did you spend the most amount of time (social media, texting, etc.)? Is that where you want to spend the most amount of your device time?

ii. Where are spots you can cut back on device time?

iii. Set a goal for the amount of time you want to spend on your phone tomorrow. See if you can stick to it!

How to Figure Out If Your Phone Tracks Your Activity:

Many of our fancy-schmancy phones today actually track our activity for us (how convenient—if not a little creepy). If you have a smartphone (e.g., an iPhone), you can usually check to see if your phone is tracking your activity by heading to the Settings on your phone. There, you'll likely see the option to look at something like Screen Time. Click on that, and there you have it: a minute-by-minute analysis of how much time you're spending on your phone (and what, exactly, you're doing!). As part of this Internet Challenge, use the information to set a goal for the amount of time you want to spend on your phone (and where, specifically, you might want to cut back). I know you can do it!

CLOSING
THE DIGITAL CITIZEN CODE

Congratulations—you've officially finished *ReThink the Internet*! You're now an internet whiz: ready to take on the world of technology, a step ahead of any traps or pitfalls the digital world may try to place in your path. But before you go, it's time to make your internet pledge: your pledge to digital leadership, to spreading kindness—not hate—online, and making the internet a fun, happy place to be. 'Cause, hey, if you can make the digital world even a little less sucky, you can make a big impact.

Read the Digital Citizen Code on the next page, and make your pledge:

I [NAME HERE], MAKE THIS PLEDGE TO THE INTERNET.

I pledge to uphold my duty to be a positive digital citizen, and recognize that everything I say or do online impacts my fellow digital citizens.

In that vein, I promise to choose kindness and watch what I say online, because words matter.

I pledge to be an informed internet user and pass on to others only that which I'm sure is true.

I won't let the internet get the better of me—I pledge to think before I type, because everything I post or send represents who I am.

I promise to be an upstander when I see something that isn't right.

I will use technology to bring out the best in who I am and empower those around me—as an activist, changemaker, creator, and dreamer.

I pledge to never let my phone replace, instead of enhance, my life.

Finally, I pledge to pass it on—and better the internet, one message at a time.

(Sign here) x _____

145

CLOSING INTERNET CHALLENGE

Congratulations on completing this book, and making your internet pledge! To celebrate, film and share a video of you reading the Digital Citizen Code—and making your pledge—on social media. Don't forget to use the hashtag "#MakingMyInternetPledge"!

ACKNOWLEDGMENTS

Writing this book has always been a dream of mine, a dream that stemmed from my many experiences meeting and talking with the world's young people. Over my eight-year career as an anti-hate activist, I have met hundreds, if not thousands, of young people globally, and it was their courageous stories, their belief in the possibility of a better internet, and their urging to make that vision concrete that led to the creation of this book. First and foremost, I'd like to thank all of you, my fellow Gen Zers, for being brave in your dream of a better digital reality, and for inspiring me to bring that reality to life.

I am eternally grateful to my editor, Jill Santopolo, for helping me make digital literacy concepts fun and interesting for young readers. In my very first conversation with Jill, I knew instantly that I had found someone who not only understood why this book was important, but also my vision for a book that my fellow young people would love. Jill's insights and perspective are the reason this book isn't just informative, but accessible and engaging. More generally, her support in writing this book—both literary and personal—was simply invaluable. Thank you also to the Penguin Random House and Philomel Books team, especially Cheryl Eissing and Talia Benamy.

Thank you to my literary agent, Kristin van Ogtrop, who,

from the very beginning, believed in the promise and potential of this book. I approached her with the idea of writing a book that could both educate and make an impact, and it is only with her perspective, encouragement, and support that I was able to realize both. It was a privilege to be able to work with her and the incredible Inkwell team.

Thank you to the entire ReThink team—for your support as I pursued this project, and for serving as a constant source of inspiration and motivation in writing this book. Your work to build an online world that is safer and kinder, and to help cultivate a new generation of digital citizens, is at the core of what this book is about.

Thank you to the many people—friends and family—who supported me throughout the creative process, especially my parents, Bhanu and Neel Prabhu, who encouraged me to go down rabbit holes and experiment with any and all ideas (and who kept me well-fed). Thank you also to a personal mentor and inspiration of mine, Reshma Saujani, who helped me navigate—and ultimately, find my place in—the publishing world. And thank you to Nick Maxwell, who supported me at my highs and my lows.

And last—but certainly not least—thank you to the many groups and entities that have rallied around ReThink the Internet's vision; your support of this book has not only been crucial to its creation, but to the change we hope to inspire. Thank you especially to the Elevate Prize Foundation, the Social Innovation and Change Initiative, and the Bryan Cameron Education Foundation. Your belief in this work means the world.

RETHINK THE INTERNET
COMPANION GUIDE

WELCOME AND WHY THIS BOOK IS IMPORTANT

Hi there! Whether you're a parent, educator, guardian, friend, or simply a reader hoping to engage more deeply with the lessons in this book, welcome to *ReThink the Internet*! I'm so thrilled you're here. Your presence here is incredibly important—not only because it will facilitate and reinforce the lessons and tools this book teaches, but because it will also allow you to begin practicing that tricky skill of talking about and critically evaluating the internet with teenagers. (If you just shuddered, you're not alone!) As you likely know, there's an art to talking to Gen Z about the internet and technology, whether it's phone use or how to carefully evaluate information online, and it's my hope that this companion guide can help you master it.

Why have these conversations at all? you might be wondering. Well, in an ever-connected and digitally driven world, it's important that your reader knows not only how to use the internet—which, if I had to guess, they likely have down to a T—but also how to use it in a way that's smart and safe. Digital know-how and digital literacy are not the same, and moving from the former to the latter is what enables digital citizens to be critical, responsible consumers of this newly online world, to benefit from the good and avoid (or potentially take on!) the bad. The sad fact is that most of today's youth, despite having been born into a wired world, were never taught much about it, never equipped with a digital tool kit. This book is that tool kit—a one-stop-shop guide to the internet that, along with your help, will ensure your reader is ready to navigate the digital world with confidence. (For a lengthier description of this book and my background, flip to the "Welcome to This Book" section.)

In the pages that follow, you'll find supporting material for each chapter of this book. Each section corresponds to one chapter and will include: 1) a brief recap of that chapter's story; 2) a rundown of the digital literacy concepts explored (and why they matter); 3) a series of discussion questions and reflections—tied to both the story and real life—that will enhance your reader's takeaways from the chapter; and 4) some brief practical advice on supporting your reader as they complete the chapter's Internet Challenge. Please feel free to use the material as a guide, not a rule: engage with the questions that resonate the most with you and your reader, and feel free to try variations of the Internet Challenges (especially if you think they'll be better tailored to your reader's interests). Together, we can craft an experience that's meaningful for your reader.

Let's go ahead and get started! I hope you enjoy supporting your reader in reading this book as much as I enjoyed writing it. Thank you for joining this *ReThink the Internet* journey!

Trisha Prabhu

CHAPTER 1: The Post Heard Round the World

Chapter Recap: In chapter 1, "The Post Heard Round the World," readers meet Melinda Skirt-Shirts, a bubbly, creative young woman and aspiring fashion designer. After learning that her mom is remarrying, Melinda is tasked with her dream job: designing her mom's wedding dress! Unfortunately, when she finds herself creatively blocked—unable to envision the perfect dress—Melinda decides to get inspired by snapping pictures of the folks around her, whether friends or people she doesn't know, and sharing her fashion critiques on the social media platform FashionGram. Though well-intentioned, the approach backfires, with her mom questioning whether she's up to the job and one of her best friends, Priya, feeling disappointed in her behavior.

Digital Tool Kit Skills: This chapter aims to teach the skill of **responsible digital citizenship.** The key conceptual takeaways are:

- When you get a device, though it may not feel like it, you actually join a larger digital community (of which you become a member, or citizen).
- Everything you say or do can reach and impact all of the folks in that community.
- Given the above, it's your responsibility to be on your best behavior online, in service of the larger community. This is called "good digital citizenship," and it not only is the right thing to do, but it also makes for a better digital world.

153

(Remember, you're a part of that world, so it should matter to you!)

Discussion Questions/Reflections:

1. Do you think Melinda intended to hurt the people she took pictures of? Why or why not? What does your answer tell us about what it takes to be a good digital citizen?
2. Priya cautioned Melinda against her actions, but didn't ultimately stop her. As a digital citizen herself, do you think that Priya's actions were enough? Is there anything else Priya could've done?
3. What's a time you saw something online that disappointed you or seemed like an example of poor digital citizenship? Why? What could you have done in response?

Chapter 1 Internet Challenge: This chapter's Internet Challenge encourages readers to: 1) ask a friend's permission before posting a picture with them on social media (including the hashtag "#AlwaysImportantToAsk") and 2) challenge at least five friends to do the same. To help your reader complete the challenge, brainstorm a friend they can ask and additional friends they can challenge. You can even help them find or take a great picture!

CHAPTER 2: Internet People Are Real People Too

Chapter Recap: In chapter 2, "Internet People Are Real People Too," readers follow along as Brody McNewKid starts his first day at a new school in Washington, DC, where Brody and his family have recently moved from Louisville, Kentucky. Brody feels isolated and out of place . . . that is, until he meets Fatima Talkie, a friendly chatterbox who shares his love of the outdoors. But Fatima's excitement at making a new friend quickly fades when, after school, she learns that her parents are getting a divorce. So when Brody then unknowingly sends her some pictures of him and his family on a hike, Fatima can't take it—angry, she lashes out at him through her texts and on social media, leaving Brody confused and hurt. Fatima later realizes she let her phone get the better of her—and feels terrible. She apologizes to Brody, promising herself she'll never again say something online that she wouldn't say to someone's face.

Digital Tool Kit Skills: This chapter is designed to teach readers how easy it is to let your words get away from you on your phone . . . and how, when done repeatedly, such behavior can become cyberbullying. The key conceptual takeaways are:

- We all say things we regret, but this is especially easy to do on the internet, when you're looking at a screen and not someone's face.
- The term "cyberbullying" refers to repeatedly harassing or hurting someone online. Cyberbullying is super sucky, because no one wins: victims' feelings are hurt, and cyberbullies compromise on their values.
- You can avoid cyberbullying by practicing a simple mantra: if you wouldn't say it to someone in person, don't say it online.

Discussion Questions/Reflections:

1. How do you think Fatima's messages to Brody affected him? What do you think that tells us about online bullying and its impacts?

2. Brody's sister, Sarah, tells him that "sometimes, people need our forgiveness when they least deserve it." What do you think she meant by that? What were some of the advantages of Brody assuming the best and de-escalating his conversation with Fatima?

3. Think about a time a friend posted or shared something on social media that they'd likely never say in person. Why do you think they did that?

Chapter 2 Internet Challenge: The chapter 2 Internet Challenge asks readers to catch themselves the next time they're about to say something questionable online . . . and to share a picture on social media of the most important people in their lives (using the hashtag "#InternetPositivity")—as a reminder that internet people are real people too. To support your reader in this challenge: 1) ask them to identify a time they were about to share something online but then decided against it (no judgment!) and 2) help brainstorm which special folks your reader can feature on their social media (maybe it's you)!

CHAPTER 3: It's Not Always True?!

Chapter Recap: In chapter 3, "It's Not Always True?!," readers meet Sherlock Solver, an aspiring detective whose dreams of important mystery work have yet to be realized. In fact, apart from the recent disappearance of Dustin Dieber, his mom's celebrity crush (yuck!), there's almost nothing to investigate! Pair that with the fact that his best friends are away, and it looks like it's going to be an incredibly boring summer. Lucky for Sherlock, he soon learns that one of his best friends, Isaiah Imallergic, is actually back in town . . . but their reunion is ruined when Isaiah has an allergic reaction to what his mom thought was wheat-free chicken parmesan. Mrs. Solver is shocked to learn that her source—*Dr. Rong's Food Encyclopedia*—isn't very reliable (Dr. Rong isn't even a doctor!). Sherlock's shocked to learn that his mom could actually be wrong . . . and that sometimes the "facts" you have might not be right. That new, powerful lesson ultimately leads to Sherlock's first big break in detective work: uncovering the fact that Dustin Dieber was never missing after all! (In fact, the whole thing was just a joke started by a fan on social media.) Case closed!

Digital Tool Kit Skills: This chapter aims to show readers how ubiquitous mis- and disinformation can be—and just how easily anyone (even adults!) can be fooled. The key conceptual takeaways are:

- You might think that all of the information floating around on the internet is true, but with no "internet police," plenty of it is more fiction than fact! In short: be careful not to trust everything you see or read online.

- Know the different types of rotten info! "Misinformation" refers to unreliable information that's spread accidentally (e.g., Sherlock's mom sharing an article on Dustin's supposed disappearance), while "disinformation" refers to false information spread with the intent to deceive.

- Whenever you're online and looking at some information, be a digital detective by: 1) checking the source, 2) noting the date, 3) avoiding anonymous (or unknown) sources of information, and 4) keeping an eye out for bias!

Discussion Questions/Reflections:

1. Let's try to categorize the different types of false information in this chapter. How would you describe the initial post intending to trick folks into thinking Dustin had disappeared? What about any posts Mrs. Solver shared on social media about Dr. Rong's "wheat-free" chicken parmesan recipe?

2. Using the digital detective tips, think about how Mrs. Solver should've evaluated the news she saw on SocialGram about Dustin's disappearance. Is the source here reliable? Does the information seem biased or extreme?

3. Think back to a time you saw or read some fishy information on the internet. What was it? Did you know it was false or inaccurate? If so, how did you know? If not, how could you have possibly detected that?

Chapter 3 Internet Challenge: This chapter's Internet Challenge encourages readers to "get on the case" themselves! Readers are asked to use the chapter's digital detective tips to evaluate a source online, ultimately deciding if the source is reliable and the content trustworthy. To assist your reader in this challenge, help them find an interesting source to look at. Then, encourage them to share their findings with you, probing their reasoning and celebrating their work!

CHAPTER 4: Are You *Sure* You Want to Post That?

Chapter Recap: In chapter 4, "Are You *Sure* You Want To Post That?," readers get to know AJ Commander, an ambitious seventh-grade student. AJ already knows what he wants to be when he grows up: the president of the United States! As far-off as that may be, though, AJ's first foray into politics is already here: he's running to be the president of his school's student council. With his sister, Ayesha, as his campaign manager, some snazzy suits, and a creative slogan ("Vote for AJ: your wish is his . . . Command!"), he should be ready to go . . . but AJ's still worried he might lose, especially because he's going up against Igor Bossy, one of the most popular guys at school. So when AJ has a chance to watch his No. 1 political hero—the local mayor, Mr. Hugh Mouth—at a virtual Q and A before the town's mayoral election, he's all ears! Unfortunately, the event takes a terrible turn when supporters of Mr. Mouth's opponent, Diane Shift, join the event. Frustrated—and insulated by his digital environment—Mr. Mouth forgets to think before he types, ultimately sending a series of rude messages to Shift's supporters. He later tries to apologize, but it's too late: the messages are trending, and now he's the one losing support! For AJ, the lesson is clear: always pause, review, and rethink before you type.

Digital Tool Kit Skills: This chapter aims to teach readers the importance of **being intentional with their words**—offline and especially online. The key conceptual takeaways are:

- Even though the internet has changed (for example, there are a ton more folks on it now than a few decades ago!), **internet design has not changed with it.** As a result, elements of that design—from thinking that we can always rely on a DELETE button, to looking at a screen and not someone's face—can make it seem like our words online don't matter.

- **That's not true: it's so important to think before you type.** Take that DELETE button, for example—even if you try to delete a snarky comment, in today's digital world, there's a good chance it's already been screenshotted and saved.

- Don't try your luck! **By taking just a few moments to pause, review, and rethink, you can outsmart the internet.**

Discussion Questions/Reflections:

1. A big part of this chapter's story is, of course, Mr. Mouth's virtual Q and A! Let's take a moment to look back at and critically reflect on it. What digital design elements of the Q and A do you think made it especially easy for Mr. Mouth to get carried away (and later, increased the damage done by his comments)?

2. Think about a time you said something you regretted online. What were you thinking? How were you feeling? What do your answers suggest about what creates tough digital situations and how you can rethink them?

3. A popular resource to help rethink offensive messages online is the ReThink app (created by yours truly)! Check it out at rethinkwords.com. Based on what we've learned in this chapter, why do you think an app that asks you to "rethink" before you post is so effective? After that, download it and get right on rethinking!

Chapter 4 Internet Challenge: The chapter 4 Internet Challenge encourages readers to celebrate when they successfully rethink a questionable message by sharing a post with one of the provided custom captions emphasizing the importance of choosing to #RethinkBeforeYouType. To support your reader as they take on this challenge, ask to chat with them about the message that they decided to rethink, exploring their reasoning. Then, help them choose the best caption for their post!

CHAPTER 5: If You See Something, Say Something

Chapter Recap: In chapter 5, "If You See Something, Say Something," readers are introduced to Kristin Artiste, a middle school math whiz and an extremely talented artist. For Kristin, painting isn't just cool, it's a form of self-expression—a way to bring her feelings to life. So as she experiences her first crush—on the incredibly handsome Juan Lipsmacker—she decides to paint a portrait of Juan (complete with stars, hearts, and fireworks—everything Kristin feels when she looks at him!). Unfortunately, several girls at school, including the troublemaking Lisa Rabblerouser, have noticed Kristin's crush and decide to sabotage her: one day at school, when Kristin leaves her phone unlocked at her desk, Lisa uses the opportunity to find and post a picture of Juan's portrait to SocialGram! Kristin has never been so humiliated, and thinks there's no way she could possibly ever live it down . . . until Juan actually takes a stand against Lisa's actions, condemning the harassment. By saying something, Juan quickly turns the tide at school, and Kristin suddenly finds herself being complimented for her incredible art skills! As Juan himself says, "It was the right thing to do."

Digital Tool Kit Skills: This chapter aims to show readers the incredible power of being an upstander; that is, using one's voice to advocate for kindness rather than hate. The key conceptual takeaways are:

- The internet is far from perfect, so there's a good chance that even if you're on your best behavior, others won't be. **But that doesn't mean you don't have a role to play**: by being an **upstander**, you can help build a more respectful internet.
- Whether it's a more obvious form of harassment or something that's subtle, by taking a stand, you can not only stop hate in that given situation, but also **set a powerful example for your friends, family, and community.**
- Lots of young people worry that being an upstander isn't cool, **but that couldn't be further from the truth!** There are so many awesome upstanders out there, from Greta

Thunberg to Malala Yousafzai. Like them, **you can act on behalf of a better world**.

Discussion Questions/Reflections:

1. Let's break down one of the most crucial parts of this story: when Kristin is confronted by Juan's friend, Tony. How exactly did Juan go about being an upstander—what aspects of his language, behavior, etc., accomplished that goal? What was the immediate reaction from the crowd watching—and what do you think that conveys about upstanders' influence?

2. Being an upstander is about taking a stand to do the right thing, but never about escalating a situation that could be dangerous or harmful. How would you differentiate between the two?

3. Has there ever been a time when you behaved like an upstander? How did you take a stand? Alternatively, has there been a time when you could've been an upstander but chose not to be? Why didn't you?

Chapter 5 Internet Challenge: The chapter 5 Internet Challenge gives readers the chance to be an upstander! Readers are encouraged to post or share our custom-made *ReThink the Internet* upstander graphic on their favorite social media platform, using the caption to explain why they choose to be an upstander ("I choose to be an Upstander because . . . "). Support your reader as they complete this challenge by helping them brainstorm reasons why being an upstander is important to them, specifically. Then, help them craft an individualized caption for their post!

163

CHAPTER 6: You Can Change the World (Really!)

Chapter Recap: In chapter 6, "You Can Change the World (Really!)," readers are introduced to Tanya Techguru, a fifth grader and technology genius with a passion for building the coolest robots, apps, and software out there. With her computer, Grace (named after acclaimed computer scientist Grace Hopper), Tanya has built everything from the Scoop-O-Rama, which scoops the perfect scoop of ice cream, to a "Candy for All" rocket launcher, which, after takeoff, drops candy all over town! Unfortunately, though, being a tech genius makes it hard for Tanya to fit in at school, where she's teased for her interests—especially because she's a girl. Infuriated by the teasing and the sexist stereotypes, Tanya decides to launch Operation Women Rising (OWR), a social media site for women who love tech and creation—just like her! After weeks of hard work, OWR is ready for launch, and after some trepidation, Tanya has the site go live. The next morning, she wakes to over a thousand users, including the famous movie star Hottie Hotshot's daughter, Karishma Hotshot! Above all, the experience shows Tanya the power of using her skills for good—of being a technology activist! Tanya no longer wants to build things that are just "cool"; she wants to build things that make a positive impact.

Digital Tool Kit Skills: This chapter aims to show readers that technology and the internet aren't all bad—and that **by embracing tech, they can actually make the world a better place.** The key conceptual takeaways are:

- The internet has its problems, but that doesn't mean that we should hate on it! In fact, technology and the internet can be used **in endless ways (there's no one "right" way!)** to change the world.

- The best way to use tech to make a positive impact is to apply **your unique skills**—whether in art or sports—to **issue areas you care about**, like protecting the environment or helping the disabled community, and using **tech to support that work**. As an example: I applied my scientific research skills to the issue of cyberbullying, using computer programming to build an app that stops online hate in its tracks!

Discussion Questions/Reflections:

1. In the story, Tanya comes to identify as an "activist." What does it mean to be an activist? By the end of the story, how has Tanya embracing this identity come to change her technology interests?

2. Fill in the blank: "I actually think technology and the internet are awesome because they _____ _____ if you use them in the right way."

3. Have you ever had an idea to leverage technology for good? What was it? What problem did you hope to solve?

Chapter 6 Internet Challenge: The chapter 6 Internet Challenge encourages readers to get their start at being a technology-powered changemaker by brainstorming a way that they can use technology for good, whether by starting an online fundraiser or creating a video to draw attention to an important issue. Support your reader with this challenge by helping them brainstorm how they, individually, can leverage technology for good, given their skills and interests. Then check in on their progress as they work to complete the challenge!

CHAPTER 7: #IRL

Chapter Recap: In chapter 7, "#IRL," readers get to know seventh-grade best friends Calvin McBestie and Paul Fonelover. Unfortunately, Calvin and Paul's best friendship is facing one of its biggest tests to date: the arrival of Paul's first phone. For as long as he can remember, Calvin has done pretty much everything with Paul, from playing basketball on the school team, to competing in video game tournaments at the local video game store, VideoWorld. In fact, they're so rarely seen without one another that they're often jointly called "Palvin"! But when Paul finally gets a phone—leaving Calvin alone without one—Calvin starts to notice some changes in his friend: Paul's late to basketball practice and class, makes excuses to avoid hanging out with Calvin, and seems to spend all his time *on his phone*! Calvin's hurt, but tries to ignore the behavior, telling himself he's being "clingy." But the last straw is when Calvin catches Paul in a lie about being unavailable to participate in a VideoWorld tournament . . . because it turns out Paul's just using the time to play the exact same game on his phone! Calvin confronts Paul, who admits he's been obsessed with his phone . . . and has lost track of what really matters. He apologizes, and Calvin and Paul head out to shoot some hoops—best friends again.

Digital Tool Kit Skills: This chapter aims to show readers that there's a real downside to spending too much time on their phones . . . and that **phone use is at its best when it enhances, rather than replaces, their lives.** The key conceptual takeaways are:

- Being on your phone all the time has a number of negative impacts, starting with the fact that **too much phone use just isn't good for you**: it can make it harder for you to fall asleep, and is even associated with being less happy or fulfilled. (Your reader can use the skills they learned in chapter 3 to back up all these claims with information on the internet.)
- Even worse, too much phone use means that **your phone can start to replace your life**, taking the place of all the things that really matter, like friends and family.
- By **being conscious and thoughtful about your phone use** (for example, by monitoring how much time you spend on your phone), you can ensure that it doesn't take over your life.

Discussion Questions/Reflections:

1. Paul spending all of his time on his new phone didn't just affect his relationship with Calvin, it impacted everything from his schoolwork to his other interests. Can you find and

point out these effects in the chapter? Why do they seem to be concerning?

2. Let's now reflect a bit on Paul's intentions: Do you think Paul meant to hurt Calvin by spending all of that time on his phone? What does the answer suggest about how to use a phone responsibly?

3. Have you ever caught yourself spending too much time on your phone? What were you doing? How did all of that phone use make you feel?

Chapter 7 Internet Challenge: The chapter 7 Internet Challenge asks readers to hold themselves personally accountable for the time they're spending on their phones by tracking their screen time, including where they're spending the most time on their device. Support your reader as they complete this challenge by going over their results with them, then helping them set a goal of where and how much to cut back. Help them stick to that goal!